THE DELTICS

The Deltics

A SYMPOSIUM

Cecil J. Allen   G. F. Fiennes   Roger Ford

B. A. Haresnape   Brian Perren

LONDON

IAN ALLAN LTD

First published 1972
Second edition 1977
Reprinted 1978

ISBN 0 7110 0799 3

© Ian Allan 1972 and 1977

*Published by Ian Allan Ltd, Shepperton, Surrey, and printed in the United
Kingdom by Cox & Wyman Ltd, London, Fakenham and Reading*

Contents

The Prototype

by ROGER FORD

IN 1955, diesel power on British tracks was a rarity. Granted, the standard 350hp shunter had been proliferating since before World War II, but main-line diesel motive power was still something to wonder at. On the London Midland and Southern Regions, the ex-LMS and ex-Southern diesels Nos 10000, 10001, 10201, 10202 and 10203 were building up operational experience, and the first orders of the modernisation plan had been placed for a menagerie of 14 different designs to be evaluated in service. The most powerful of these designs would weigh nearly 140 tons and put only 2,000 to 2,500hp on to its six powered axles. Diesels for export were marginally better in their power-to-weight ratio. In 1955 English Electric were building the first narrow-gauge diesel with 2,000hp installed, but even this weighed 113 tons. Then in October of that year Sir George Nelson unveiled at English Electric's Preston factory the biggest single step forward of the whole of the BR Modernisation Programme, the prototype Deltic locomotive.

This is not to overestimate the importance of the Deltic or the magnitude of its impact. At its birth it was the most powerful diesel locomotive in the world; and though the title was increasingly qualified over the years as, first, multiple-units and then conventional diesel-hydraulic and electric locomotives overtook it in installed power, the Deltic remained unequalled on its home ground 15 years later, save for a single 4,000hp prototype some ten years its junior. In 1955, however, when 2,000hp main-line units were still three years away, the Deltic provided 3,300hp in a 106-ton Co-Co layout, compared with the eight-axle 130-ton plus monsters to come. In its time the Deltic advanced the state of the art as much as the Comet airliner or the first Mini motor-car in their own fields.

In design and construction the prototype Deltic was not, in fact, all that remarkable save for the engines. The steel superstructure was a welded one-piece load-bearing structure already used for several export designs. The generators running at engine speed (1,500rpm) were considerably faster than those fitted to conventional 850rpm engines, but like the traction motors were of basically conventional

7

design. The engines themselves, however, were unique, and they alone made possible the Deltic's combination of the two key parameters of locomotive engineering. Before the Deltic there had been powerful locomotives (steam in particular) and there had been lightweight locomotives; the Deltic was the first really powerful lightweight locomotive. It was entirely appropriate that the prototype and the succeeding production units should always be known by the name of the engine.

The diesel engine which made the locomotive possible had its genesis in prewar Germany. For long-range aircraft the diesel engine with its low fuel consumption and independence of troublesome electrics was an attractive proposition—if it could be made light and powerful enough. In 1929, Junkers Motorenbau flew the first of its aircraft diesel engines. This developed into the Jumo 205, which ultimately powered a number of civil and wartime aircraft, mainly long-range transport and reconnaissance planes. To produce a compression ignition engine with aircraft standards of power-to-weight demanded a radical approach to the subject. The solution was a six-cylinder vertical opposed-piston two-stroke engine. It weighed under 2lb per horsepower. The successful formula is familiar—it was in fact the description of one bank of a Deltic.

The year following the first flight of the Junkers engine, a British aero-engine firm began negotiations to buy the know-how from Junkers. The firm was D. Napier & Son. By 1934 Napiers had built two versions of the Jumo, but apart from test flights nothing came of the venture, partly because of the demand for Napier petrol engines created by the rearmament programme. During the war Napiers made only one type of engine—the mighty Sabre, a 24-cylinder H form engine which ultimately produced well in excess of 2,000hp. Meeting the tremendous demand for the Sabre added another link in the chain of events leading up to the Deltic locomotive. In 1942, the Government asked Mr George Nelson to reorganise the Napier Works for mass production of the Sabre engine; shortly afterwards Nelson's English Electric Group took over Napiers and he became Managing Director for the next seven years.

George Nelson, later Sir George, later still first Baron Nelson of Stafford, became Managing Director of the infant English Electric Company in 1930. Under him the company weathered the depression and began to grow. Several of the companies which had come together to create English Electric had been associated with other forms of rail traction than steam, starting with the first experimental electrified lines. Their experience came together in the English Electric Traction Division, which was responsible for a number of prewar electrification schemes both at home and overseas.

From this base it also began to develop a series of diesel-electric locomotives, the first real commercial success being the initial orders for the 350hp diesel shunters which were to become the BR standard. After the war the Division built larger locomotives, the 6-cylinder shunter engine growing into 12- and 16-cylinder models which would ultimately give over 3,000hp. At home, main-line orders were limited to power equipments for a number of prototypes, but several Commonwealth and other overseas railways bought fleets of English Electric locomotives as the start of main-line dieselisation programmes.

The final link was an Admiralty requirement for a high-powered diesel engine to power fast patrol boats, replacing petrol engines with their heavy maintenance requirements and fire risk. The Admiralty placed the development contract for this engine with English Electric, who in turn gave it to their new subsidiary— Napiers—and so the Deltic engine was born. It was an 18-cylinder opposed-piston two-stroke, with its 18 cylinders arranged in three banks of six having a common crankshaft at each corner of the resulting triangular engine. Extensive use of light alloys in the construction made the engine light, while the unusual cylinder arrangement made it compact and very smooth-running. It took its name from its triangular cross-section, which resembled an inverted Greek letter *delta* (although some pedant later pointed out that this was in fact the Arabic *nabla*, and that the engine should really have been called the "Nablic"). Development on the engine began in 1947, the first complete unit ran in 1950, and two years later sea trials began with the engine (in mechanically scavenge-blown form) producing 2,500hp.

Although intended as a marine engine, other applications were sought for the Deltic, where a high power output from a lightweight, compact engine would offset the relatively high initial cost of such a sophisticated power unit. One such application was rail traction. There is no doubt that Nelson was the catalyst that sparked off the Deltic locomotive. He saw what the Deltic could mean in rail traction terms, even with the engine greatly derated to give the necessary life and reliability. And once the joint project of Napiers and his Traction Division was established he pushed it along with all the force of his undoubtedly forceful character. Finally he "signed" the cheque for the engine to be traction-rated and a prototype built. There was to be no experimenting with a single engine installed in a small prototype;

the first Deltic locomotive was to prove the point straightaway, and it would be the most powerful diesel in the world. The £250,000 private venture had begun.

The Deltic represented the fusion of Napier's infectious optimism with the slightly reactionary, hard-won diesel traction experience of English Electric. There was no problem in building a locomotive to take the engines; but the engines had to be acceptable to the railway engineering establishment. The power was there in abundance, but this would have to be traded-off against increased service life. The critical factor was time between overhauls. After at least 10,000hr in service the conventional four-stroke 850rpm diesel requires its first overhaul, which is virtually a top overhaul and is done *in situ*. Major overhauls with the engine removed from the locomotive should not be required until after many tens of thousands of hours. In its original marine form the Deltic engine gave 2,500hp for a 1,000hr life. Calculations showed that derating to a continuous 1,650hp for traction duties should give a time between overhauls of 6,000 hours.

To counter this relatively short life (and because it was impossible to overhaul Deltic engines either *in situ* or in steam shed conditions) it was decided that overhaul by replacement would be adopted, with the engines being taken out of the locomotive when servicing became necessary and returned to the factory for attention while refurbished engines were installed. Between overhauls there was, in fact, very little to do on the engine—only injector changes at 2,000hr. The importance of this to the hard-pressed running engineer was later reflected in the heartfelt listing of what the Deltic engine didn't have by an engineer with both Deltic and normal engines in his care: no valves, no tappets, no cylinder-head joints and no rocker-box covers. The Deltic as a "sealed power-box" concept was to make a major contribution to the intensive working which lay in the future.

Having made its *début* and been shown to British Railways engineers and running staff, preliminary running trials with the prototype began in November 1955, on the London Midland Region between Euston and Liverpool, mainly on fast freight trains. Early in 1956 it was withdrawn from service for a number of minor modifications to be made, and on returning to service took part in series of tests aimed at establishing the limits of Deltic performance. These tests took place during August and September, and were organised jointly by the owners and the British Transport Commission. The test results, based on over 5,000 miles of testing, were subsequently published in BTC Bulletin No 19.

The scene for the trials was the section of the LMR between

Carlisle and Skipton and the results recorded by the Region's mobile test plant gave a foretaste of the new standards of performance the Deltic was to set. The bare figures gave a tractive effort of 45,550lb held for 2min without slip, equivalent to 2,650 rail hp. Thermal efficiency at 40mph was 27.5 per cent, and on one engine there was 1,270hp at the drawbar at 25mph. The actual test trips made the point more directly. On one of the runs a train of 20 coaches, grossing 642 tons, was taken over the test route with the engines at maximum power for as much as was possible within the prescribed speed limits. The sustained drawbar hp was around 2,200 and the 15 miles from Ormside to Ais Gill, largely at 1 in 100 up, were covered at an average speed of 56mph and a maximum of 50mph. Fuel consumption for the run worked out at 1.27 gal/mile. The test team recorded that there had been no defects of any significance in the 5,000 miles of testing and noted the low maintenance requirements of the engines. The only criticism was that the engines were considered noisy when idling, which might prove objectionable in stations.

After the trials the Deltic was put on to passenger services between Euston and Liverpool working the "Merseyside Express" from Liverpool to London and returning with the "Shamrock". In January 1957, it began a short spell between London and Carlisle, but by May it had reverted to the London to Liverpool service and the next month the schedule was modified to include an additional round trip between London and Crewe daily. This schedule was designed to show that the claims for the intensive running made possible through low maintenance requirements were valid. It began with the 00.37 from Crewe to Euston, followed by the 07.55 from Euston to Liverpool, the 14.10 from Liverpool to Euston and finally the 19.20 Euston to Crewe; 703½ miles a day, six days a week.

Little has been said here about speed; indeed, the Deltic *forte* has always been the rapid acceleration up to the route maximum. But there are reasons for thinking that on one occasion a very high speed was reached by the prototype. The traction motors were originally geared for 90mph, and this was subsequently increased to 105mph. However, on one run over Shap in the early days a burst of speed on the down-grade resulted in the armature banding on all six traction motors bursting through overspeeding; it might well have taken a speed up to 130mph to produce this effect, though there is no positive proof that so high a maximum was actually reached.

It was during the prototype testing that the famous Deltic feature, the 8hr engine change, emerged. This soon became a staple part of the English Electric propaganda in the enthusiastic times when the sale of the production units was being negotiated. But those who subsequently had to operate the production fleet were to be disappointed, for while the Deltic engines could be changed quickly, the 8hr change was a possible achievement rather than a routine matter, and, moreover, was based on a prototype with a liberal supply of Napier and English Electric engineers. Yet somehow the 8hr change crept into print and stayed to become part of Deltic mythology.

It was easy to see how the fast changes were achieved on the prototype. In the event of engine trouble leading to a shut-down the riding representative would begin disconnecting the pipes, wiring and so on leading to the engine, so that on arrival at the depot the roof section was removed and little work was required to lift out the diesel generator unit. In these conditions, and with practised men, it was indeed possible to change an engine in a single shift. When the production fleet was in service, however, Doncaster Works would generally offer a "by return" engine change with a failed locomotive despatched from its home depot on, say, a Monday afternoon, and returned ready for service on the following Wednesday morning.

British Railways buy the Deltics

by G. F. FIENNES

WHEN YOU GO shopping be sure you know what it is you want to buy, then buy it. That is not a bad system for the High Street. It is a better one still in Swindon, Crewe or Doncaster Works.

It has been a pity that railways—to write a classic understatement—did not shop for locomotives like that. First the engineers, like the Stephensons and Brunel, then the mechanical engineers, down to Churchward and Gresley, kept their shops full of what the customers *could have*. It was not always what the customer *wanted*. Worse than this, often enough the customer didn't know what he wanted out of a locomotive in terms of speed, punctuality and cost. And often enough his ignorance did not matter much. To have an engine which would lick the pants off Euston in the race to the North was good clean fun for Kings Cross, but little more than that. It did not touch the question of survival. That came many decades later, with competition from motorways and the air.

The question of the survival of the Inter-City services began to loom ahead in the early 1950s. Stuart Ward and I were at Liverpool Street under A. R. Dunbar; I was Assistant Superintendent and Stuart was Head of the Passenger Section. We were having fun, sneaking the first batch of steam Britannia Pacifics by stealth from under Sir Michael Barrington-Ward's nose. He tried to stop it when he got to know; but he got to know too late—that is, when the timetable was already in the printer's hands. And so we had for a month or two on the Great Eastern the fastest train in Britain. A photo of the "Broadsman" on our Christmas card went with every circumstance of derision to Kings Cross, Paddington, Euston and York. We got those Britannias by being in the shop when it opened, and because they were in the shop.

But going shopping like that for over a hundred years had brought railways to a brink where they were on the slippery slope of a permanent Inter-City traffic decline and at an increasing rate. There was some excuse for the party from the British Transport Commission which went to America and came back saying: "The Yanks will be out of the express passenger business by 1970. We won't be far

13

behind". Contrariwise, at about the same time Stuart and I were
trying to get down on paper what we really wanted in terms of speed,
knowing that unless we got speed, end-to-end speed or *vitesse commerciale*, as the French would say, it would be no use having low
cost or punctuality. And when we had decided what the job was, then
and then only would we go shopping for the tool.

For competition with the road it worked out very simply. The
graph in the accompanying diagram, drawn at the time and just as

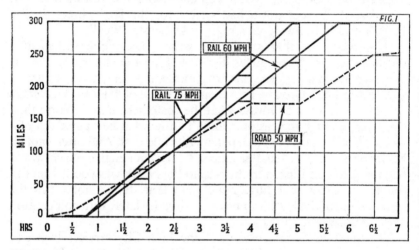

Fig. 1. Comparative speed of road and rail in the future.

valid today, plots a road journey by dual carriageway between two
large cities. By road it assumes a speed of 15mph for ¾hr at the start,
an average of 50mph on the open road, and a stop for a meal after
four hours. Against this are set two rail journeys at speeds of 60 and
75mph. These assume that the passenger will occupy ¾hr at the start
of his journey reaching his main-line station and getting into the train,
having left a margin for delays on the road and rail feeder; and that
he will take a ¼hr at the end of the journey between station and
destination. The answer stuck out a mile. An average of 60mph
would not do. *Vitesse Commerciale* was, and is, around 75.

At that speed we should be well in the competitive running for
distances upwards of 70 miles, and as some more sums told us, we
should not run into crushing competition from the air until we got
up to 300 miles. The job then was 75mph wherever we had, or chose
to compete with, dual carriageways. Then and only then we did our
sums about the tool to be used.

At this time the BTC was buying off the peg any diesels that any manufacturer had on offer. And a motley and largely useless collection they were! For the Great Eastern we did our best, insisting that only the highest horsepower on offer would do, namely 2,000. Soon after that Stuart and I went to the Great Northern and I made public our findings with the kind of phrase which has endeared me to my bosses through life: "The policy of building diesels of 2,000hp lies in ruins around us. Nothing less than well over 3,000hp under the bonnet will do."

In 1957 therefore, in the presence of diesels of only 2,000hp, we set off to plan main-line electrification out of Kings Cross, but I find I wrote to Stuart on November 5, 1959:

"*Modernisation and Electrification of East Coast Main Line*
The meeting with the BTC about GN Electrification went, on the surface, extremely well. Messrs Grand, Ratter and Warter were obviously in favour of the proposals and in fact were pressing for greater speed in execution, talking of a target date of about 1967. Mr Donachy also—he did not see any reason why it should not be extended immediately to Edinburgh.

Sir Cecil Weir was obviously uncommitted; Sir Leonard Sinclair, while not declaring himself, did mutter about diesels and may be taken to be against.

The Chairman, after being apparently in favour throughout the meeting and in fact saying 'when you talk about completion in 1970 ... I begin to yawn', summed up that we should present projects for route modernisation as quickly as possible in fairly large parcels, but should indicate with each whether any component of the expenditure is an integral part of the electrification. From this I concluded that he wants the Commission still to have room for manoeuvre, and is not committed to supporting electrification at this stage."

And we were in a hurry. Passengers in numbers and receipts were declining. We had to fill the gap. In 1958 we had introduced the Hoyle steam timetable, about which was written: "The Great Northern is getting better performances out of its elderly locomotives than ever it did in the prewar years ... the timetables refer with unconscious humour to 'semi-fast' trains, many of which are booked at averages of over 60mph between stops". But of course this was nowhere near good enough. Further in anticipation of electrification the engineers were demanding possessions of the line and consequent temporary speed restrictions which would cost us 12min extra between Kings Cross and Shaftholme Junction.

As between a steam Pacific in good fettle and a 2,000hp diesel there was nothing to choose, and traffic was still declining. So, like the Psalmist, we lifted up our eyes unto the hills of Westmorland where there were rumours of secret preparation to try out a Goliath of a locomotive. It took us quite a long time to find out what it was all about. This was of course, in the tradition, not only of Gresley who kept No 10000 in wraps as his "hush-hush" locomotive, but also of the splendid rivalry between Kings Cross and the Euston Confederacy. When we did find out, one fact denied—or confirmed— all my principles about the buying what is in the shop. Goliath was to have 3,300hp under the bonnet. And the London Midland were going to use him as a Goliath, hauling ponderous trains over enormous hills. "It will", they said, "take 650 tons up 1 in 120 at 40 miles an hour".

"They" said also–the magnificent "they" who look at projects standing on their heads in order to make it appear that they don't turn them down—that "it won't be permitted north of York; it can use one platform only at Kings Cross; it has high-speed engines against which our face is immutably set; and it has a top speed of 105mph which you can't use".

This last phrase settled it. Goliath was not a giant bullock; he was a racehorse. And Chief Civil Engineer A. K. "Sandy" Terris was at that very time equipping long stretches of the GN Main Line for 100mph in anticipation of electrification. Between 100 and 105mph, given a good sight of the distants—what's the odds?

Leaving aside the physical prohibitions we went straight into preparing a financial case; what we could earn and what we could save with a fleet of Deltics. In considering what more we might earn we had to remember that we had not then in British Railways the modern sophisticated marketing techniques. We were still in the empirical world which allowed that from past experience a suburban electrification produced 100 per cent more revenue. That same world had no experience of the effect of diesel traction on Inter-City revenue. Moreover, we were looking on the Deltics as a holding operation, bought to arrest a decline in revenue until we could electrify. We came quickly enough to the conclusion that it would be difficult to make a particular figure for increased revenue stick to the BTC's enquiring mind, and that it would weaken the case for electrification if it did. We decided to base our case on economies.

The task was no small one. The price for one Deltic was over £200,000. The small fleet which we wanted would cost over £4m.

The prototype Deltic pulls out of Rugby with a Liverpool–
Euston express.   [*C. P. Walker*

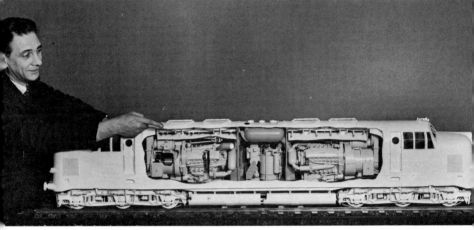

Top: A broadside view of the prototype Deltic at the head of the 14.10 Liverpool–Euston approaching Rugby on April 29, 1958. 　　　　　　　　　　　　*[M. Mensing*

Above: A cut-away model of the prototype Deltic, which was displayed at a British trade fair in New York. One of the eighteen-cylinder engines was sectioned to show a line of cylinders in the triangular 'Deltic' formation, from which the engine and locomotive derived their name; the main generator and radiator fan gearbox were also sectioned.

Opposite, top: The prototype Deltic on the LMR, passing Edge Hill with a Liverpool–Euston express. 　　*[Eric Treacy*

Opposite, centre: The prototype Deltic on the Eastern Region undergoing freight haulage trials; it was photographed passing Potters Bar on March 21, 1959 heading a dynamometer car and a rake of fifty loaded coal wagons.

[H. Gordon Tidey

Opposite, foot: The Deltic prototype during its special tests over the Leeds–Carlisle line in 1956; it is seen at Skipton on August 22, with the BR Mobile Test Unit. 　　　*[T. K. Widd*

Above: The prototype Deltic in ER express service; it heads the 12.20 Hull–Kings Cross through Hornsey on April 12, 1960.
[*M. Edwards*

Below: In the export shop window — the prototype Deltic in Glasgow Central heading a special train laid on for a Canadian trade mission in 1957.

Near the end of the road — the prototype Deltic on route to the Science Museum on Sunday April 28, 1963 passes Hanger Lane, in West London.

[*M. Pope*

Last resting place for the Deltic prototype is the Transport Gallery at London's Science Museum, in South Kensington.　　[*Science Museum*

How the production Deltics might have looked — a bodyform with raked-back nose and slight wraparound to the cab windows evolved by design consultants Wilkes & Ashmore. Note the air intake on the top of nose and headboard incorporating body between tail lights. The nose tapers inwards towards the front whilst the lower body skirt remains constant in width to provide a foot platform at the front end. The cab windows and doors are linked by an aluminium paint scheme. *[British Rail*

A production series Deltic in its original two-tone green livery with the BR emblem centralised on the bodyside.

Close-up of a production series Deltic front-end and bogie.
[*Brian Haresnape*

No 9000 in original livery, experimentally fitted with an
electric flashing light above the buffer beam as a warning
device for trials on the ER.   [*Sam Lambert*

Since they were to be a stopgap for ten years only, we thought it prudent to amortise capital at a rate of over £400,000 a year. The mechanical engineers forecast that the cost of maintenance would be double that of a "normal" diesel. In all we faced a brick wall a million pounds a year high.

Nevertheless we had shown in the Britannia timetable what even moderate acceleration and tight diagramming would save. So, back we went to the Timing and Diagramming Section. It is a matter of history that they saved the money. The diagrams required 23 Deltics each running 200,000 miles a year, a figure beyond the dreams of British operators until then. The 23 would be in place of 55 locomotives of less power and stamina, would avoid running frequent relief trains and would save a satisfying number of footplate and shed staff. We had got up the wall and the trumpets all sounded for us.

We sounded them in fact ourselves. Behind the wall were still the damned disinheriting countenances mouthing about high-speed engines, route availability and 100mph. The makers, English Electric, bless them, did the hard work. They undertook a maintenance contract and they streamlined the shape down to the RA7 category, which meant that they could run over pretty well any main-line in Britain. We at Great Northern House marched round sounding off like Joshua until suddenly the wall fell flat on its face and we were in. In the interests of good order and discipline the BTC cut the number from 23 to 22. The makers promised delivery in 1960 and 1961. The person who wants something is always stronger than the person who doesn't want him to have it—if he wants it enough.

A couple of months later, in July 1958, the prototype was running tests up the fells out of Carlisle. *Trains Illustrated* commented: "The Eastern Region has chosen well". It took us another six months to get our hooks on her, and then she ran into trouble. The steam heating boiler used mysteriously to shut down, till someone found that if the driver opened the throttle in a tunnel she gulped all the air in the neighbourhood. She "became derailed" in Hornsey Loco and had to go for modifications to bogies. And of course she had to carve her way by knocking down a few things in more than one platform at Kings Cross.

But by mid-February 1959, she was working the 08.20 from Kings Cross as far as Doncaster and the 13.35 back. In March she ran from London to Newcastle in 3hrs 50min. I rode a number of times on her (or should I say "in her"? This dilemma of expression has never been resolved since Harold Hoyle named a train "The Fair Maid of Perth" and had to rename it in a subsequent timetable). Driver Bill

Hoole took a conversion course and admitted when no one of importance was listening that she climbed Stoke Bank faster than a Class 8
Pacific.

In short we knew that we were on a winner; and the rest of this
part of the story is one of impatience. Traffic was still declining and
one prototype buttered no parsnips. So let me quote a memo:

"Line Traffic Manager to S. D. Ward, August 20, 1959:
       Deltic East Coast express passenger service
Many thanks. Generally convincing. The only point is the timing of
accelerations. On programme we shall have ten Deltics by September
1960 and sixteen by Christmas. Delay will have to be justified by,
firstly, evidence of late deliveries which we shall not get before the
winter timetable 1960 is prepared; and, secondly, by the training
programme in some detail if we are to show cause why we do not
put some locomotives into public service with accelerated timings in
September and a further batch with a winter supplement.

In spite of the general prosperity of the country main-line passenger
traffics are declining and two of our defences against this must be
speed and publicity—both of which are inherent in the Deltics.

Is there any reason why we should not prepare a scheme for
selected trains to be accelerated on a date to be decided in, say,
March 1960, when the prospect of deliveries should be firm?"

And another memo on December 14, 1959:
"The deputation from Dundee expressed their points about mail on
the 19.30 from Kings Cross very reasonably. The booked times, of
course, are late for organising first delivery and the actual time makes
it frequently an impossibility.

The deputation agreed not to press the matter as an immediate
project on the understanding:

1. That Deltic locomotives would take over the diagram after
delivery and driver training, thereby ensuring far better punctuality
in the present timings. This I said I thought would be reasonable in
June if the manufacturers made their delivery date of April.

2. That the timetable accelerations of Deltic traction would be
carried out before the bad weather next winter, by which I meant,
although I did not say so, with the winter timetable 1960.

Please proceed on these lines dealing with Scotland as may be
necessary."

April came and went. No swallow made that summer or that
autumn or that winter. So the next memo is dated January 13, 1960:

"Mr Harrison telephoned to say that he had a note from English Electric forecasting the delivery of three Deltics for certain by the end of February and they would catch up with their latest forecast of delivery dates by the autumn.

He has asked for a note what difference it is going to make to our plans, to which I have replied firstly that if they catch up with delivery dates by the autumn, ie October, there will be no change in our plans; if they do not catch up we shall have to introduce the accelerated business services in stages, some in the winter timetable and the remainder in the November and January supplements."

And then of course the rats got at it. Another memo dated May 2, 1961 says:

"Mr Harrison telephoned this morning about the rate of delivery of Deltics and said that the General Manager had met Sir George Nelson, who told him they could not, with the bogie modifications, retain the delivery of the Deltics as planned for the next month or two and also modify the bogies on the Type 3 on the Great Eastern. Mr Harrison asked, in view of the GE summer timetable commitments, that we should accept reduction in the rate of the Deltic deliveries. I said:

1. That the continued preference to the Great Eastern was something to which we had become accustomed but not reconciled.

2. That I said recently to the Board, and had had the point of view accepted, that we should accelerate no trains in the autumn timetable, for which the locomotives had not been in our hands for at least four months.

3. That I did not, as East Coast co-ordinator, accept any delay in the delivery of Deltics which would prejudice the winter timetable without consulting the North Eastern and Scottish Regions, who would be most unlikely to have more sympathy for the Great Eastern than the Great Northern had.

4. I suggested therefore that the rate of delivery of Deltics should remain unprejudiced until the sixth locomotive was delivered, ie until May instead of, as he suggested, by the end of June. After that time, speaking for the Great Northern, we were prepared to have an intermission for the benefit of the Great Eastern provided that the rate of delivery of the Deltics was then stepped up so that the programme was restored by October."

I was just there for the Harvest Festival on September 11, 1961, when we accelerated a bunch of trains. Among them was the 19.30

down "Aberdonian", fulfilling our promise to John Strachey, MP, just a year late. In passing I can never resist the crack that whereas railways measure their punctuality in minutes late, their suppliers measure theirs in months or years.

And then I was caught up in a chariot of fire and landed in 222 Marylebone Road. Others made the East Coast what it is, a profitable rival of the West Coast, securing as large a proportion or larger of the Inter-City traffic as the Euston electrification.

The Production Deltics

by ROGER FORD

WHILE THE PROTOTYPE was building up the hours, English Electric was working hard behind the scenes, pressing British Railways for a production order, and with Nelson still taking an active part in the selling. The Deltic engine introduced a new concept to the railways—overhaul by replacement—and as the talks continued English Electric's proposals reflected this basic factor in the operation of the Deltic.

Essentially, the contract for production units would be in two parts. The purchase of the locomotives would be quite straightforward, but would also cover the maintenance of the fleet and the overhaul of the engines for an initial period of five years.

This maintenance contract introduced an important development: it would be geared to the performance of the locomotives. English Electric would be paid to supervise the maintenance of the Deltics, and Napiers would overhaul the engines. However, if the Deltics fell short of their scheduled mileage a penalty factor would come into operation which would reduce the sum paid for the maintenance and engine overhauls.

Eventually, in the spring of 1958, British Railways could resist this tempting offer no longer, and took the plunge. Twenty-two production Deltics would be ordered for the Eastern Region, where they would replace 55 steam locomotives—and, more to the point, would enable the impatient Mr G. F. Fiennes really to accelerate his trains. Delivery would begin in 1960 and be completed by 1961. A year after the contract was signed, the Eastern Region got the prototype for route trials on scheduled services between London and Doncaster. It also took part in some braking tests which showed that it could stop in a shorter distance than the steam locomotives it was due to replace. But what really impressed (as always) was not its stopping but its going; for example, as described elsewhere in this book, an average of 88mph for the $16\frac{1}{2}$ miles up to Stoke Summit with a trailing load of 355 tons. In 1961, when the first production units were nearing completion, the prototype returned to English Electric's Vulcan Works with over 400,000 hard-working miles on the clock, and stayed there until it found a final home in the Science Museum in London.

The production units differed in appearance and constructional details from the prototype. To begin with they were a surprising 7 tons lighter than the already lightweight original; they were 3ft 6in longer; the bogies were the same as English Electric's standard Class 37 design, which was itself a development of those on the Deltic prototype but with a slightly shorter wheelbase; and the main generators were geared down to run at 1,125rpm instead of directly driven, to reduce the chance of flashovers. The external appearance was different, too, as the result of a prolonged struggle between the engineers and the nascent Design Panel of the British Railways Board (*see following chapter*). The prototype had been distinctive with its headlights and yellow chevrons on the blue body-work. To 1970 eyes it may have had the same brash design as its contemporary cars, but in its own time there is no doubt that this drew attention to this powerful diesel, which was what was needed.

The compromise between function and style in the production Deltics has, in the writer's opinion, produced the most handsome diesel of the modernisation era. The designers were denied curved windows, raked verticals and the pointless sculpturing of the Western Region diesel-hydraulics, but they have given the design a series of compound curves where other nose designs had sharp edges, and have devised a livery that has slimmed down the bodywork. The result is functional, powerful and virtually ageless. These sentiments on styling may be reactionary, but it is significant that until the birth of the HST those arbiters of taste—the BRB publicity men—invariably put a Deltic at the head of any advertised non-electric train which had to appear fast and powerful. Even a poster for a parcels service showed the train to be Deltic-hauled!

Because of delays in construction, the first Deltics to be delivered did not reach Finsbury Park until March 1961. All but two made their appearance in that year and No 9021 brought the fleet up to strength at the end of April 1962. Between the euphoria of 1958, when the talk was of a minimum of 5,000hr time between overhauls for the Deltic rail traction engine, increasing to 10,000, and the *début* of the production units, the TBO had fallen to a more realistic 4,000hr. This was not a setback, however, because this time fitted in exactly with the strenuous schedules which had been devised for the Deltics; 4,000hr represented one year's running. Because the overhauls had to be staggered during the winter months, some engines would have to come out of service before their true TBO was reached, reducing the average for the fleet over a year to 3,700hr per engine.

Despite the 400,000 miles achieved by the prototype, the engines were still not absolutely right. Before delivery began a complete power unit, including air ducts, exhaust tubing and silencers, radiator and fan, was set up in Napier's test-house and run for 1,000hr at simulated traction loadings. This showed up a number of faults, in particular wear on splined shafts. A subsequent 200hr test with a complete locomotive on the test tank brought to light what was to be one of the worst Deltic problems—severe cavitation corrosion of the cylinder liners. The spline problem was being cured as the first locomotive engines were being assembled, but the liner troubles were to drag on for some time, although ameliorated by the use of an inhibitor in the coolant.

The first months of service running showed up more troubles. Faulty welds in the drum tanks, which acted as collectors for the three exhaust manifolds, cracked, and because the tanks also accumulated a fair amount of unburnt lubricating oil this leaked out. So the tanks were fitted with drains to remove this oil, which often blocked, leaving a risk of fire. The engines were fitted with overspeed *and* underspeed switches, and the latter proved too sensitive to vibration and frequently shut down a good engine. And there was more severe liner corrosion, with several liners failing through fatigue and causing blow-backs into the cooling system. Redesign of these and other components was put in hand.

Why were there problems like this in a production series based on such extensive prototype testing? In my opinion the explanation is a simple one. Whereas the later prototypes operated in a diesel-oriented railway environment, the prototype Deltic was running on the same schedules as those of steam locomotives or at best lower-powered diesels. As a result, for much of its life the prototype was running to easy timings even when hauling heavy trains, and often with yellow warning signals ahead. Thus while it was putting in the hours and the miles, it was not being driven hard to accelerated schedules as the later production units were. Thus its reliability and maintenance requirements could not be extrapolated to the hard life on the Eastern, and inevitably for the first few months there were relatively serious teething troubles. But they *were* teething troubles, and the penalty clauses in the maintenance contract had the effect of concentrating the manufacturer's mind wonderfully. In addition the repair by replacement philosophy minimised the effects of engine problems.

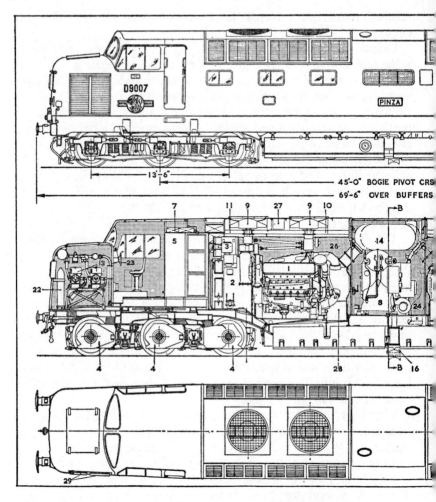

Fig. 2. Scale line drawing showing (*top*) the side and end elevations, (*centre*) a cutaway side view and (*foot*) a plan elevation.

1 Napier "Deltic" engine
2 Main generator
3 Auxiliary generator
4 Traction motors
5 Control cubicles
6 Batteries
7 Resistances
8 Train heating boiler
9 Radiator fans
10 Coolant radiator

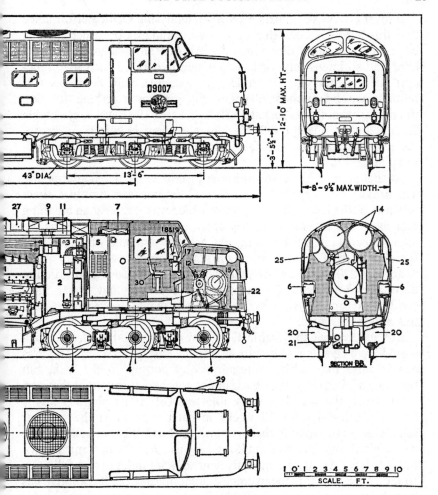

11 Lubricating oil radiators	**21** Water tanks, 620gal
12 Compressor	**22** CO_2 cylinders
13 Exhausters	**23** Handbrake
14 Silencer	**24** Water tank filler duct
15 Traction motor blower	**25** Engine air filter and duct
16 Water pick-up scoop	**26** Fan gearbox and drives
17 Master controller	**27** Header tank
18 Vacuum brake valve	**28** Lubricating oil tank
19 Air brake valve	**29** Traction motor oil filters
20 Fuel tanks, 940gal	**30** Driver's seat

It must always be remembered when analysing Deltic performance that this unique locomotive set its own standards by which it must be judged. No other diesel fleet on British Railways has worked so hard and so intensively, or has consistently covered such high mileages. In the first year of service, for example, with deliveries still taking place and unscheduled engine changes due to teething troubles, the mileage run from August 1961, to August 1962, was a creditable 2.75m; and as Cecil J. Allen's logs elsewhere in this book prove, the miles covered by the Deltic locomotives are invariably hardworking and fast.

At this point it is worth outlining just what Deltic standards are. The heavier trains hauled to accelerated timings were simply a direct function of the installed horsepower, which was greater than anything that had gone before. From the operator's point of view it was the intensive working which was the real achievement, and which justified spending some £200,000 apiece on new locomotives. The key parameter was 220,000 miles per year, which was the baseline for calculations associated with the maintenance contract, and under ideal conditions each locomotive in the fleet would have approached this annual distance.

But in practice the Deltic fleet never reached this ideal, which would have been equivalent to an annual mileage of 4.8m. This was not because the Deltics were physically not up to the task, but because the necessary work was simply not there throughout the year.

However, the fleet has been able to work at its planned highly intensive schedules for 12 weeks in each year when the summer schedules are in force; in these conditions the Deltics have shown that the original concept was sound. As early as 1963, the fleet mileage for this 12 weeks was over 1m, equivalent to 4.5m miles over a full year. In fact, over the years the average annual mileage per locomotive has been between 150,000 and 180,000. It was a performance such as this that the maintenance contract guaranteed, and with such a small fleet responsible for such high mileages any unscheduled excess could have had a serious effect on availability—and on the manufacturer's balance sheet.

During 1962 the development of better pistons and liners continued against a background of expected troubles with the existing versions of these components, in the form of loose piston crowns and cracked liners. More significantly the first two engines passed the 4,000hr mark and were removed for performance testing before stripping and overhaul. The power output was on the curve although the fuel consumption was up slightly, reflecting the state of the injectors and the blower. While piston and liner problems were being overcome a new problem arose—fatigue in coolant pump drive shafts, which was overcome with changes in material and finish specifications, although fatigue troubles with the various drive shafts in the Deltic engine were to continue for another couple of years.

While the engineers were sorting out the engines which made it all possible, operational running was showing up problems which were not connected with mechanical or electrical performance. One such was noise. The British Transport Commission's test report on the prototype had commented adversely on the noise level around the locomotive and the production units were not noticeably quieter. Among the people upset by the noise were the drivers themselves, who soon complained about the noise level in the cab. Several remedies were tried. The obvious one—ear muffs—had to be abandoned because they were uncomfortable and, so it was said, because the drivers found that they couldn't "read" the road by ear in the dark.

In the end full height acoustic damping panels were fitted immediately behind the driver's and second man's positions with a padded curtain which could be drawn across to close the space between them. While this lowered the noise level, it made the cab very cramped by any standards, and the seats became less comfortable than before because their backs were bolted flat against the acoustic panel. Noise in stations was not a serious problem, because engines were shut down as soon as the trains had stopped. Stopping itself *was* noisy, however, for as the engine ran down it reached a point where the gears in the phasing case oscillated wildly, causing a very loud chattering noise without any apparent warning. Otherwise as far as the customer was concerned most of the sound and fury took place outside the station, while from inside the train it was reduced to a fairly quiet hum.

Once they were in service it rapidly became apparent that the Deltics made nonsense of the old belief that the coming of diesel and electric traction had taken the skill out of driving. In fact they put a premium on a sensitive touch, as far as the controller was concerned, particularly when starting. The design of the load regulator, which matches engine output to the power being taken from the generator, provided only a small number of contacts at the beginning of its travel. As a result a relatively small movement of the controller could run up the torque regulator in a series of coarse steps, making it very easy to put more power on to the rails than the available adhesion could cope with.

A good place from which to study this phenomenon was at the site representative's hut beside the entrance to Gasworks Tunnel at Kings Cross on a wet day. In these conditions pulling away on a Deltic with a 12-coach train became a test of skill rather than a case of merely pulling back the handle and letting it happen. In fact several drivers did get stuck in this tunnel, and at certain other points along the line, and this led to a modified design of torque regulator with additional "starting contacts" to make pulling away easier in marginal conditions.

At the other end of the speed scale the Deltics soon proved to be unsurpassed. As the tractive effort curve shows, the Deltic has a higher tractive effort than the more powerful Class 86 electric locomotive as speeds rise into the 70s. A Deltic accelerating at full power could make the yellow wheel-slip warning light flicker at over 80mph as the effortless surge of power drove it onwards.

Although there was a background of teething troubles for longer than might have been expected, they were all essentially minor, and through them all the locomotives kept accumulating the miles. This was the strong point of the fleet; it kept on running and the performance—in terms of reliability and engine life—kept on improving. A key factor in this was, of course, the fact that the manufacturer was penalised for any loss of availability under the maintenance contract and also that the Deltic engine was continually being developed throughout the 60s and into the 70s with more and more power being wrung out of the classic design. Experience from the design and development work which took the marine rating of 18-cylinder Deltic engines to all but 4,000hp, improved the much lower rated 1,650hp units working on the Eastern Region. The capacity of the electrical equipment meant that these engines could not be up-rated, but the time between overhauls has been progressively raised.

In 1966, when the first five-year maintenance contract expired, 4,000hr was assured and the first engines had begun to reach 6,000hr. The maintenance contract was then renegotiated—the original one was believed to have been uneconomic as far as English Electric were concerned. By 1968 the overhaul period was up to 5,000hr for the purposes of maintenance schedule calculations, and the average life obtained was nearer 5,500hr; round about this time the first engine reached 6,500hr.

But at this point the steady improvements in engine life came to a halt and 5,000hr remained the norm. This abrupt halt to a previously rising curve was due in part to the changing fortunes of the Deltic engine in naval use and the re-organisation of the English Electric diesel empire in the wake of the GEC–EE merger. The rapid rise of the gas turbine in naval use meant that Deltic engine sales for fast patrol boats virtually disappeared and inevitably pressure on the research and development departments eased. At the same time the Napier organisation was moved *in toto* from its Acton base to the Paxman Works at Colchester to become part of Paxman diesels. The move further disrupted design and development, and also manufacture; that was to lead to a shortage of spares which would later become sufficiently severe to take two locomotives out of service at a time waiting for engines to return from overhaul. Finally much of the research effort at Paxmans was concentrated on the build up of the new Valenta engine.

Then came the turnround and Naval demand for the Deltic engine rose as rapidly as it had fallen. By 1975 Deltic manufacture was in full swing again and more research and development effort was being applied by both Napier and BR to extending the time between overhauls of the rail traction engines to 6,000hr, a period which would fit into the extended maintenance schedules now being observed. The main obstacle to the required life was the piston plus some continuing liner difficulties (although the use of the thicker 42K liner virtually cured these). By 1976 a new design of piston with a bolted crown (a development of the Mk IV piston first proposed in 1964) was replacing the screwed-on crown in service trials and promising to give the necessary 6,000hr.

This need for extended engine life is illustrated by a comparison between the original and the 1976 Deltic maintenance programmes:

At introduction

daily	weekly	monthly	3-monthly	6-monthly	annual

1976 programme

28hr	10 working days (12 max)	40 days (48 max)	120 days (144 max)	10 monthly	20 months

With the original scheme based on a 4,000hr engine life, shopping occurred twice in a working year with a visit for bogie changing every six months between the annual engine change. Now a 6,000hr engine life is needed to provide an overhaul period coinciding with the life of two sets of bogies.

It will be seen that the two determinants of the Deltic overhaul schedule are the bogies and the engines. The lives of these parts did not improve at the same rate and by the late 1960s the maintenance schedules for the mechanical parts, the electrical equipment and the engines had got out of phase. This meant that locomotives were being taken out of service for separate attention to items which should have been dealt with at a single shopping.

In 1970/71 Doncaster works—which had been overhauling the Deltic engines since the end of the second maintenance contract in 1969, following a successful pilot scheme with the engine for the Class 23 "Baby Deltics"—had the chance to bring the maintenance schedules back into phase again. In 1970 the Deltics started to go into shops for their first major attention in nearly a decade of intensive working. This followed the introduction of electric train heating (ETH) on BR. Adapting the Deltics to ETH meant putting in new 1,000V jumper cables to take the power supply from the main generators to the train. To do this the cable ducts had to be stripped out so the opportunity was taken to rewire the locomotives. At the same time the rest of the electrical system was refurbished, including rewinding of electrical machines where required. As the engines are rebuilt at each overhaul, this rewiring and refurbishing work brought the power equipment back to zero-hours condition, good for a further 10–15 years' running. Experience with English Electric locomotives overseas, some of which have been running since the early 1950s, has shown the need for refurbishing of the mechanical parts, which do not receive regular attention, as a locomotive ages. ER has prepared a refurbishing programme for the Deltic superstructure, but whether this is implemented depends on how much longer the class is expected to run—a subject discussed later in this chapter.

Conversion of the locomotives to ETH also had the effect of improving the performance of the locomotives when starting. As explained earlier, Deltics were prone to slipping because of the rapid rise in voltage to the traction motors over a relatively small number of contacts in the torque regulator. One way round this, which some drivers employed, was to start the locomotive on one engine. As the two generators are connected in series, starting with only one engine running would effectively halve the voltage and enable the tractive effort to be applied with more finesse. With the advent of ETH, BR engineers were faced with the need to provide sufficient volts for the train heating, not only when the locomotive was on the move but also in station with the engines idling. Because the Deltic's auxiliary generator could not provide enough power for ETH the supply had to come from the main generators—hence the problem of providing enough volts for the train at idle.

The solution was to take the ETH supply off one generator and give this engine a faster idle to provide enough power. Having re-designed the control system to achieve this, it was realised that the new arrangement could be used to improve performance when starting. Now, when the controller is pulled back the engine supplying power for ETH, which is already running faster, picks up first, giving the same voltage characteristics to the traction motors as starting on one engine. A simple solution—although one requiring some complex changes to the control circuitry—to the problem of the Deltic start. It also resulted in a simpler control system. An interesting point is that both engines can supply power for ETH and take the duty in turns, depending on the direction the locomotive is travelling, to even out engine wear.

While ETH was installed, the steam-heating generators were retained for use with the steam-heated sleeper stock. As with many other locomotives the Deltics had been fitted with scoops for picking up train-heating water from steam locomotive troughs. These were finally removed on the ER in 1969/70, which meant that the Deltics had to carry extra water for the long-distance Scottish sleeper services. The additional tankage was obtained by sacrificing some fuel capacity, which leaves the Deltics with adequate fuel for a London–Edinburgh run with one diversion. With two diversions the fuel gauges could start bumping on their stops!

These changes, together with the conversion to air braking in 1967/68, inevitably reduced mileages. The "golden year" as far as mileage was concerned was 1963/64, when 3.96 million miles were run with an engine availability of 99.77 per cent. From this peak, mileage dropped for several reasons. First, the pattern of the time-table, with the concept of a busy summer timetable and a more relaxed winter being replaced by an intensive year-round service. Second, the introduction of the nominal 2,750hp Class 47s meant that they could take over certain Deltic duties. The result was that the Deltic fleet settled down to a steady 3.6–3.7 million miles annually. This gave individual annual mileages of around 168,000 and in 1975 the first locomotives began to pass the $2\frac{1}{4}$ million miles mark. During 1974 and 1975, the spares shortage already referred to resulted in one or two locomotives being out of service for long periods and the latest annual fleet mileages reflect this.

In the middle of 1976, when this chapter was being completed, the Deltics were running as intensively—in terms of operation if not sheer fleet mileage—as when they entered service. But in 1976 the first threat to Deltic supremacy on the East Coast main line for 15 years was at last in sight in the form of production High Speed Trains leaving Crewe and Derby works for working-up trials between York and Newcastle. While the first trains were destined for the Western Region, in mid 1977 the Eastern Region would start to receive its 32 HSTs. The East Coast racing ground, which has enabled the Deltics to put up such an impressive performance, is ideally suited to 125mph HST running, with the time between London and Edinburgh scheduled to fall to 4½hr. With the advent of such performance it might be thought that a 21-year-old design, and a small fleet at that, would follow other non-standard BR diesels to the scrap heap. That this will not be the case is due to three factors—the Deltic's continuing status as BR's most powerful diesels; a smaller ER HST fleet than originally planned; and the uncertainty over future investment in BR.

Initially the ER wanted 42 HST sets, 32 for the ECML and 10 for Humberside services. Had this requirement been met the Deltics would have gone on to parcels and sleeper traffic. Apart from the one sleeper which is a Deltic timing, putting Deltics on to sleepers would improve overall locomotive utilisation by freeing Class 47s for freight working at night. Clearly not all the 22-strong fleet would be required for this work.

Financial stringency meant that the ER was given an initial allocation of only 32 HSTs. So, with the introduction of HSTs into ER squadron service, the Deltics were now to take over Humberside services and York semi-fasts in addition to the sleeper and parcels traffic. With new Mk III coaches and short train sets Deltic haulage should be able to provide an acceptable service on these routes in an HST environment. Once again the full fleet would not be required and presumably the new size of fleet would be arrived at by withdrawing locomotives failed for lack of spares or requiring heavy maintenance.

The survival of the class was also aided by the permanent derating of the Class 47 Brush Sulzer locomotives to 2,580hp and the 300hp or so required by the electric train heating on new coaching stock. As a result, even given a clear run, a Class 47 will be 1–2min down on a Deltic schedule. This further strengthens the case for retaining the Deltics in service. From the start it has been well known that the Deltics cost more to run than conventional units. While the depot cost is slightly less (as would be expected) the workshop bill is definitely higher. Yet when the costs are added up and divided by fleet mileages the difference between ER Class 47s and Class 55s is only a fraction of a penny with no clear advantage either way. But the Class 47 costs are a fleet average and it is now accepted that high-

The steam-to-diesel transition on the ER: a Deltic alongside Class J50 0–6–0T No 68988 at Leeds Central on September 7, 1963.

[*J. M. Rayner*

The Deltics acquire names: No 9007 *Pinza* at York in August, 1961 heading a Newcastle–Kings Cross express after working down to Tyneside earlier in the day with the 'Flying Scotsman' from Kings Cross.

[*L. Metcalfe*

Above: Yellow warning panels are applied to the noses of the Deltics; No 9016, as yet unnamed, accelerates the down 'White Rose' through Doncaster on May 14, 1963.

[*J. S. Whiteley*]

Below: Still unnamed No 9008 passes Ardsley motive power depot with the down 'White Rose Pullman', at this date a mixture of old and new Pullmans.

[*Eric Treacy*]

Steam-age headboard on a Deltic: No 9009 *Alycidon* at
Edinburgh Waverley with the up 'Flying Scotsman'.

[*Eric Treacy*

Before the 100 mph Deltic era: nowadays one would never
see short-wheelbase vans marshalled next to the locomotive
as they were on the down 'Aberdonian', passing Potters
Bar on July 6, 1961 behind No 9004.   [*J. F. Aylard*

One of the first Deltics to be named after a regiment, No 9008 *The Green Howards*, at York with the 17.05 Kings Cross–Newcastle on October 3, 1964.   [*Brian Stephenson*

The ornate winged thistle 'Flying Scotsman' emblem devised and worn by Deltics on this duty for a period is seen on No 9013 *The Black Watch* passing York with the up train.

[*Eric Treacy*

Above: To improve their audibility warning horns were for a time mounted on the roof of the driver's cab of No 9020 *Nimbus* (Finsbury Park depot's favourite among the class); it is seen here at Wortley South, Leeds, on the up 'Queen of Scots'.

[*Eric Treacy*

Below: Broadside of No 9012 *Crepello* in present-day blue livery, with the warning horns in their now standard place on the nose in front of the cab windows; it was photographed at Hadley Wood on the 16.00 Kings Cross—Edinburgh on March 2, 1971.

[*J. H. Cooper-Smith*

No 9015 *Tulyar* restarts its engines after a brief turnround pause at Kings Cross yard in August, 1970.

[*J. H. Cooper-Smith*

The Deltic is still a useful traction unit on only one engine; only one was operative on April 10, 1971 when No 9004 *Queen's Own Highlander* brought in the 10.40 Kings Cross—Newcastle express parcels.

[*S. Creer*

speed passenger work places the greater strain on a locomotive. When the cost-per-mile calculations are based on passenger service, Class 47s already derated and struggling to keep to Deltic timings, with ETH further sapping their strength, the balance swings decisively in favour of the Class 55s as the hammering suffered by the Class 47s takes its toll. So on its own ground the Deltic is cheaper per mile *and* provides 700hp more. Not surprisingly the ER engineering and operating departments have a lot of time for their "stop-gap" fleet of veterans!

The future of the Deltics thus became fairly clear. From mid 1977 the ER would start to get its HSTs, but at a reduced production rate which would extend delivery through to the end of 1978. As soon as a large enough proportion of the HST fleet was available to make the disruption of mixed 125/100mph running viable, it would enter service with the Deltics cascading on to Class 47 duties which could possibly be accelerated. Around the end of 1978 full HST running would start and the Deltic fleet would take over the duties already described. Here, if the ER maintained its policy of ever sharper schedules, they would remain in service until further HSTs were delivered. In the best case these would follow the ER's first 32 through the shops with delivery through 1979 and the Deltics going on to secondary services in 1980. The earliest date for phasing out the Deltic fleet is 1980–82 and it is clear that the decision to withdraw the class will be taken when the running cost becomes too great for the value of the service and the extra power provided. And of course, the low intensity of secondary services will significantly reduce the Deltics' present advantage.

Many people have asked why the class could not be used to up-grade another route—North-East/South-West is the prime candidate. There are three reasons why this is not part of current thinking. One, the railways still hope to get many more HSTs and NE/SW would be an early recipient. Two, the BRB officially considers the difficulties, setting up the new facilities and staff training, associated with operating a unique class away from established depots not worth the advantage. And three, the ER values the Deltics too highly and would be very loth to let them go.

As the discussion of the Deltics' future has shown, the future of express passenger services is made uncertain by financial factors outside the Railways' control. In the midst of all this uncertainty the Deltic still stands out, providing the operator with a guaranteed 3,300hp here and now—as the class has done since 1961. Ordered as a temporary measure to cover the 10-year gap until the ER was electrified, they were paid for years ago and cannot be cancelled or postponed to save money. With the benefit of hindsight the absolute rightness of George Nelson's original concept is seen as a true diamond among the cut glass of other of diesels of the modernisation plan. With luck some of his brainchildren might just see their silver jubilee in revenue-earning service.

The Deltic Styling Controversy
by B. A. HARESNAPE

EMERGENCE of the prototype Deltic for trial running on BR lines coincided with a growing awareness, in one sector of top railway management, of the need for a sensible design policy, if the aims of the modernisation plan were to be fully achieved. A special issue of *Design* magazine for September 1955 made a well-considered plea for such a policy and in this and other ways the seeds were sown which led to the setting-up of the BR Design Panel in August 1956.

The appearance of the prototype, to eyes as yet unaccustomed to such forms of traction, was certainly startling. Because it was a private venture, the Deltic was not required to conform to the existing BR standard livery schemes. It was not long before public reaction was felt, with letters to the national press complaining about the visual appearance of the new locomotive; somewhat justified by the absurd decorations applied to a basic colour of light blue and grey. Such public reaction was to add more fuel to the fire kindling within BR top management, to ensure that the pilot scheme diesels then being planned would have proper consideration given to their appearance design.

To be fair, it was the livery rather than the actual bodyform of the prototype machine which provoked public criticism. To have chosen such an insipid powder-blue and pale grey was bad enough, but to embellish this with an unrelated scheme of cream chevrons and stripes was evidence enough that a true understanding of design was lacking somewhere along the line. As one letter to an editor at the time put it, "the prototype Deltic rivals a Zulu warrior in full war dress". Analysis of the livery scheme would point to someone's desire to impart speed to a shape as ponderous as an elephant. The chevrons at the nose-ends cheated the eye into disregarding the true bulk of this feature, whilst the lining along the bodysides, finished as arrow-heads each end, emphasised the length and disguised the depth. Unfortunately the two applications conflicted visually whenever the locomotive was viewed from the typical three-quarter angle.

An early requirement of the new Design Panel was that it should advise upon the livery and appearance of the new pilot scheme diesel locomotives. This was in itself a difficult enough task for a newly-created team, but one made all the more problematical in some cases by the directive that each locomotive builder was to be given a fairly free hand to display ideas and features for possible future standardisation. Not one of the pilot scheme designs can—upon reflection—be considered as aesthetically successful; in much the same way that a number have proved technically weak into the bargain. The late George Williams, as the first Design Officer, had the unenviable task of welding together the traditional engineering approach (still somewhat steam-biased in certain areas of top management) and the novel approach—so far as BR was concerned—of the professional industrial designer, with the ultimate aim of creating a design environment in which aesthetic and ergonomic aspects would receive attention right from the start of each new engineering concept. Inevitably some early hostility and suspicion was aroused and it was to take Williams several years to overcome these reactions; meanwhile the appearance of the pilot scheme diesels suffered accordingly.

The decision to order 22 Deltics for service on the East Coast main-line was accordingly seen by George Williams as a challenge to produce a real improvement upon the prototype, which he had often upheld as a poor example of applied styling. He had not forgotten the public reaction that the prototype had evoked, and here was the chance of a practical reply—or so it seemed at the time.

From the start, it was clear that no fundamental changes were to be made to the locomotive layout. For one thing the Deltic was a very compact package, with little room to spare within the British loading gauge. In addition, it was going to be necessary to improve upon the somewhat restricted route availability of the prototype, which could not negotiate curves of less than 6 chains, and which was prevented from operating in Scotland by its bodyshape. The cab layout and nose-ends of the prototype followed standard English Electric practice (it should be remembered that the company had an eye on the world market, not just British requirements) and there seemed little sense in making any major changes for 22 locomotives.

First practical steps taken by the Design Panel included appointment of a consultant industrial designer, and examination of the prototype. The designer chosen was E. G. M. Wilkes, of Wilkes & Ashmore, who also advised on the Brush Type 2, the Derby and BCW Type 2s, the Brush Type 4 and the Beyer-Peacock Hymek. Together with George Williams, he made a thorough inspection of the prototype, at Hornsey shed ER, and reported back in due course his basic recommendations for design improvements. Apart from the obvious shortcomings of the livery application, concern was voiced at the bulky appearance of the machine and at the restricted forward visibility caused by the huge nose-ends. It was felt that the bodyform in general was capable of considerable refinement without basic alteration of layout.

Accepting the limitations created by the need to retain the nose-ends, Wilkes drew up a more aesthetically pleasing and more practical shape for this feature, which allowed for improved forward visibility. By increasing the taper of the sides forward of the cab doors and above footplate level, and by raking-back the frontal plane he created a "fast" shape which successfully embodied details such as headcode panel and train nameboard. The lower bodyside, forward of the driving cab, remained at a greater width (within clearance limits) and was wrapped-round the front of the nose above the bufferbeam to create a footstep. The cab windows were divided into three, in place of the two on the prototype, of which the two outer panes were slightly wrapped-round to the sides.

These features, together with a revised version of the standard green BR diesel livery, were demonstrated by means of a superb large-scale model. The livery sought to reduce the depth of the bodysides (a feature which could not be avoided) by creating a visual break at approximately footplate level, using a lighter shade of green for the lower portion. The cab area, including the doors, was to be unified by an aluminium paint scheme. To improve route availability the bodysides had a gentle tumblehome from waist level.

Production schedules for the new machines were tight and there was no time to develop full-size mock-ups of the revised frontal treatment. When George Williams displayed the new proposals in model form he was dismayed to encounter unfavourable reactions both within BR and English Electric. The revised shape of the nose-ends came in for particular criticism; charges of excessive production costs were levelled against them as one objection, whilst the locomotive builders considered the metal forms involved to be too complex. When Williams countered this latter objection by observing that similar shapes were competently handled by the motor-car industry and were within the capabilities of skilled panel-beaters, his views were disregarded. Compromise won the day. A cleaned-up version of the original nose-end was adopted and the cab area remained virtually unaltered.

In retrospect, the production Deltics would have benefited from the more imaginative frontal appearance. Now that the nose-ends are dainted in overall yellow, and the bodysides are plain blue, two of the most unsatisfactory aspects of the design are emphasised. The deep bodysides and ponderous nose belittle in visual terms the top speeds and day-to-day performances of these remarkable machines. In appearance they are conservative in the extreme. One almost longs for the return of a little of the well-meant vulgarity which distinguished the prototype machine!

Living with the Deltics

by ROGER FORD

IN AN EARLIER chapter I described the Deltics' development and realisation. But what was it like to operate the Deltic fleet when diesels were still relatively new and the Eastern Region's 22 two-tone green fliers in a class apart?

In 1963 I was the junior in the London office of English Electric's Traction Division. As part of my education it was decreed that I should join the Outside Department and gain first-hand experience working on our products in the field. Although I was far from being a railway enthusiast in the usual sense of the word, I welcomed the idea. During my apprenticeship I had worked on a number of sites where power stations were being built, and had found outside department life interesting, free of restrictions, and with the advantage of carrying an extra salary allowance. Finsbury Park was the nearest depot to my home with a site office, so one Monday at the end of May I reported to the wooden hut in the sidings behind Finsbury Park sheds, where the English Electric and Napier teams lived.

At Finsbury Park we had the racehorses. Gateshead and Edinburgh had famous regiments but we had Derby winners—*Meld, Nimbus, Crepello, St Paddy* and the rest—not that we ever used the names when nice simple numbers were painted on the side. To look after our eight steeds *plus* the last of the "Baby Deltics" running at that time *plus* a generally trouble-free fleet of English Electric Class 37s and 40s we had an experienced chief site engineer, a number two who was gaining experience before going on to design or sales, and a skilled fitter. To these were added the part-time services of the three-man team which rode with the prototype DP2 while it was with us. These were all English Electric staff. Also on the site was a Napier team made up of a site representative and a fitter.

Similar but slightly smaller teams looked after the eight Scots regiments at Edinburgh and the six North-East regiments at Gateshead. All these reported to the chief Deltic representative at Doncaster, which was the overhaul and heavy repair base for the whole fleet. Bearing in mind that our own chief at Finsbury Park had been looking after a larger fleet of diesels in East Africa (including com-

39

missioning new arrivals) on his own before he came back to England, it will be seen that the terms of the maintenance contract made it worthwhile applying a lot of skilled manpower to the problems of keeping 22 Deltics running properly.

With the first batch of teething troubles under control the pressure was really on, keeping the availability of the Deltics at the top level. To achieve this result the contact point between the site team and the operators was brought forward from the depot to the station. This change was aimed at eliminating the minor faults, which could ground a locomotive if left for correction at the shed, but could be swiftly tracked down if caught as soon as the diesel arrived at the end of its run. Often these reported faults were only half faults—the mysterious non-recurring loss of power, the non-repeatable flickering warning light—faults which drivers reported to the office as they signed off or described in brief chalked messages on a control cubicle door and which could take hours to find or refute. The solution was simple, if you had the manpower; you met each Deltic-hauled train as it arrived and "debriefed" the driver. That way you could ask questions, find out which blue light had come on, what the gauges did when the engine stopped, or recognise the symptoms of a flash-over or an over-enthusiastic under-speed switch.

So for the early years of the Deltic maintenance contract there were two men stationed at Kings Cross meeting all the Deltics as they arrived. Their base was a small office behind the shed up against the face of the Gasworks Tunnel. From this hut we went into the station and had a few words with each Deltic driver before he left the cab. In most cases everything was fine but when it came to minor fault-finding the personal contact was invaluable. In one sense it was also a profitable duty as I found out one day when standing with a fellow white-overalled representative beside the cab; as the passengers streamed off the platform, an elderly traveller thanked him for the excellent trip and thrust a half-crown into his hand!

The two men at Kings Cross also kept track of the fleet movements, and checked these against the diagram in case of queries over availability. One result of this activity was the way in which No 9020 seemed to accumulate more mileage than the other Finsbury Park-based Deltics. After a few days the reason became clear. One of the representatives had "adopted" this unit, and was putting it forward for any spare duties that came along; hence the higher than average mileage, and also the non-standard colour of the buffer-beams and the selection of No 9020 for the fitting of experimental external hooters.

The day's routine on Deltic maintenance was simple. First thing in the morning any overnight failures going beyond on-the-spot attention at Kings Cross were ferried back to Finsbury Park for rectification. Minor troubles were investigated and dealt with; real problems—a blowing piston, a defective liner pressurising the coolant system, or a serious flashover, meant attention in the shed or a visit to Doncaster for an engine change. However, it was the minor problems which took up the time, because not only were they difficult to find but also, as for example a sticking contact, they could cure themselves and leave the trouble-shooter really baffled.

Because of the pressure to keep the stud running trouble-shooting began as soon as the troublesome unit arrived. With control faults as well as engine troubles it was useful to have the engines running. The routine procedure of running-up each engine to full speed, and then both engines together, was not popular with the tenants of the flats which backed on to the sidings where the testing took place. Our mechanical accompaniments to breakfast invariably produced their crop of shaken fists and inaudible mouthings before all was shut down.

Given time most troubles were tracked down, identified and rectified, but not all so easily as with the unit which refused to start after a major examination and was due to go out that afternoon. An electrician came into the site hut looking worried. Two of us put on overalls, picked up a selection of tools, and hurried over to the shed. It was indeed odd; the whole diesel seemed dead. Then inspiration struck; my chief walked back to the engine compartment and flicked over the master switch, after which we went back to the ever-present cup of tea, leaving behind a few red faces!

While at the very bottom of the site representative's ladder the living was easy, at the top the senior site engineer had the additional problem of keeping the system running smoothly. He and the local shed-master had to agree as to the responsibility for each failure, and its resulting lack of availability and loss of mileage; for under the maintenance contract it had to be somebody's fault, so that the right party to the contract paid for it. If the fault could be attributed to British Rail there was no problem, except that the site representative was supposed to supervise the maintenance work, and also had to bear in mind the need for the shed-master's co-operation. If it was the company's fault there also was no problem—except that it would be pointed out to him that he was losing the company money! The real problem occurred when agreement could not be reached, and the matter had to be referred up the chain of command in both hierarchies. So each senior site representative had to be both engineer and diplomatist.

The Napier representatives had a slightly easier time, though they wouldn't thank me for saying so! The engines gave little trouble in themselves capable of being cured on the spot, and they required little maintenance between overhauls. The troubles occurred, as ever, at the interfaces—the governors, controllers, under and over speed switches and so on. These kept our men active, but otherwise an engine either ran properly or it went back to Doncaster to be changed. One of the occasional jobs was to keep an eye on No 5905, the last of the ten "Baby Deltics" in service. These locomotives had entered service before the 3,300hp units and had run into big trouble. They were powered by a single 1,100hp nine-cylinder Deltic engine which featured turbo-charging to achieve the higher output.

After three years service a rising tide of cracked cylinder liners and failures in mechanical drives had forced all but No 5905 out of service. In the summer of 1963 it ran on unloved, uncared for and practically unserviced until one day the Napier representative found bronze bearing fragments in a filter basket and it was taken away to join its fellows in vandal-plagued retirement at Stratford. After months of neglect during which re-engining was mooted, Napier's proposals for modified engines were accepted. The refurbished locomotives entered service in 1965 and survived happily for a few more years on suburban services, where they became noted for their reliability, until their non-standard characteristics cost them their lives.

I have mentioned pressure and this was no exaggeration. Finsbury Park's honorary Deltic—English Electric's own prototype, 2,700hp No DP2, which had a Deltic superstructure and running gear, and was powered by the first English Electric 16CSVT engine, a 16-cylinder conventional four-stroke diesel rated at 2,700hp—came to the Eastern Region at the start of the summer schedules. It was promptly put to hard work filling in for the Deltics, which were being taken out of service one at a time for train-heating boiler modifications (incidentally, train-heating boilers, or rather steam-heating generators that didn't, were the bane of the diesel engineer's life; steam generator failure in an otherwise healthy locomotive was the main reason for the fall in the availability curve every winter). For the development people's benefit a return run on Sunday was added to a basic Deltic diagram and in the next eight weeks No DP2 clocked up 43,000 miles—a record for this country.

Such tight scheduling—typical of all the Deltic schedules—meant that any modifications had to be fitted in as and when they did not interfere with routine maintenance. An example was the new guards that were fitted over cooling drive shafts. To fit these you had to lie on your back on top of the engine, drill and tap the holes for the bolts, fight the pre-shaped mesh and strip steel guards into place, and finally bolt them down. Apart from the cramped working space, the cut hands and the exertion, you were also working on top of an engine nicely warmed up by its run back from Kings Cross to the shed, and with no time for it to have cooled down; and 1963 was a hot summer! Even in no more than overalls and under-pants we sweated pints, and I drank more tea than ever before or since!

But this thirst was nothing to that of certain arrivals during those early years at Kings Cross. Steam was still at work further down the line and it could happen that, if a Deltic failed, there would be no relief diesel available, and the crew would have to take over a steam engine for the last miles. For the driver this probably made a pleasant break in routine, but the second man became a fireman again, stoking an A4 and trying to catch up with timings based on 3,300hp to haul a heavy train. Seeing these firemen replacing their body fluids with pints of mild in the Caledonian Road "local" was a graphic testimony to the impact of diesel power.

Not that the drivers, contrary to the enthusiast's view, did not appreciate the new order. As many logs have shown drivers have responded to the power in hand and the challenge of the new schedules, and are still doing so. For example, one Deltic-hauled express (the "West Riding") was booked to stop at Hitchin to pick up suburban passengers for Leeds. The timing to Hitchin was easy, but by some quirk of the timetables the next 12¼ miles to Sandy had to be covered in 9½min—an average of over 70mph from a standing start. After the slow exit from the station and over the points on to the main-line even less time was available, and the handle would have to come back hard. A feature of Deltic working is the way in which the speedometer needle marches round the dial when the engines are at full power. You can see it moving all the time all the way up, unlike travel on lesser-powered diesels where the change from say 70 to 71mph is almost imperceptible. Despite this dramatic acceleration I never came across a driver who beat "par" for this Hitchin-Sandy time, but the point is everyone tried—and that is how Deltic power affected all those who had to make use of it!

What might have been

by ROGER FORD

WHEN G. F. Fiennes was whirled up in a chariot of fire to 222 Marylebone Road—or the Kremlin as it was called in my part of industry—he did not forget the Deltics. A 3,300hp locomotive now meant that even more power would soon be needed to keep BR competitive—the 75mph *vitesse commerciale*. The sums were simple. For the required speed something around 3,000hp would be needed. Add 15 per cent to reduce the load factor in the interest of reliability—say 3,450hp—plus 300hp for ETH and you got 3,750hp. As Fiennes records in *I Tried to Run a Railway*:

> I trotted along to Chief Mechanical Engineer J. F. Harrison and said: "Four thousand horsepower, please."
>
> Freddie has when shocked a disarming habit of leaning forward on his desk for a full half-minute, then slowly relaxing back in his chair and saying mildly "What?" I repeated it.
>
> He searched for words for a long time and then said: "Look, Gerry, I am up to my ears in this bloody diesel lark. The most we have now is 2,500. Sulzers are coming along with 2,750 and that's your lot."
>
> "What's wrong with the Deltics?" A bad move this.
>
> "Everything. High-speed engines are no good. They won't last—you'll see. Why not double-head?"
>
> Freddie always had a Thing about the Deltics. He could shut his eyes to the fact that they were 25 per cent more powerful than any other locomotive, that they were running double the mileage of any other and that their availability was the best in the country. However, I kept at him and was beginning to make a dent in the defences when firstly I left and secondly the Sulzer 2,750hp engine developed serious faults of design and distracted all the rude mechanicals from trying yet another New Thing.

But if the Chief Mechanical Engineer didn't want Deltic engines, their potential for making possible more powerful locomotives was not lost on the three groups of people who knew all about them—

44

English Electric Traction, Napiers and the Eastern Region. It was also not lost on *Modern Railways*, for which I was writing. Putting together apparently random pieces of information and making some back-of-envelope-calculations we postulated a diesel equivalent of the Class 86 electric locomotive to maintain competitive timings north of Crewe until electrification was completed. The later marks of AL6 (Class 86) had been uprated to 4,000hp to meet a commercial requirement for 950ton trains over the northern hills. A diesel equivalent would need 4,400hp or so to achieve the same wheel-tread horsepower—the power which could be supplied by twin turbocharged Napier T18-27B Deltic engines for only 750lb more than the pair of engines in the Class 55. In September 1966 it was all so simple. Our battle-cry was "We want 4,000hp now".

The reaction was mixed. Predictably, the BR traction hierarchy sniffed because they were in trouble with fast-running engines in the WR hydraulics and wanted the reassurance of medium-speed engines like the 4,000hp Sulzer 12LVA, which was still some years away from even prototype service. English Electric were faintly embarrassed because they had lost money on the first maintenance contract and also because as part of the traction establishment—virtual inventors of the stolid BR diesel—they still weren't too sure about small fleets of locomotives with exotic engines; although they would fight anyone who said the Deltics were less than admirable.

But someone did bite. We had talked in terms of an LMR requirement, with the locomotives perhaps being passed on to the ER as an ultimate Deltic replacement. The ER liked the idea—but straight away, please. So the following month two 'inspired' editorials appeared warning against deceleration on the ECML and calling for more power. Our first shot had been near the target—how close we would only find out ten years later.

There the "Super Deltic" rested until June 1967 when the General Manager of the ER referred to "the attractive prospect of the new 4,400hp Deltic from English Electric". It will come as no surprise to readers that the General Manager in question was G. F. Fiennes. This time we went straight to the sources for a sequel to the first article. Had it not been an indictment of the way that the BRB dominated the traction industry, and its Regions, to the railways' detriment in the 1960s, the reaction would have been amusing. We approached our sources circumspectly so as not to frighten them. If they would supply details we would protect anonymity and even submit the article for vetting. In return their mutual desire would not get swept under the carpet—and *Modern Railways* would get an exclusive.

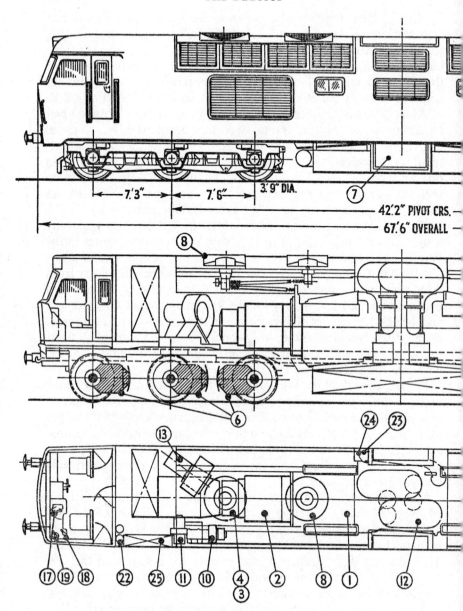

Fig. 3. The proposed "Super Deltic" 4,400hp high-speed diesel- electric locomotive of 1966.

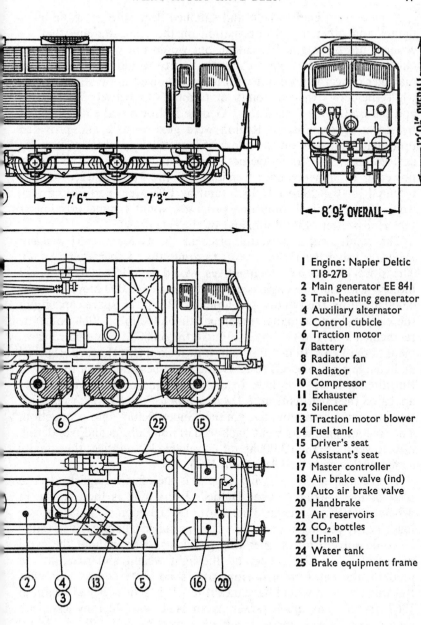

1 Engine: Napier Deltic T18-27B
2 Main generator EE 841
3 Train-heating generator
4 Auxiliary alternator
5 Control cubicle
6 Traction motor
7 Battery
8 Radiator fan
9 Radiator
10 Compressor
11 Exhauster
12 Silencer
13 Traction motor blower
14 Fuel tank
15 Driver's seat
16 Assistant's seat
17 Master controller
18 Air brake valve (ind)
19 Auto air brake valve
20 Handbrake
21 Air reservoirs
22 CO₂ bottles
23 Urinal
24 Water tank
25 Brake equipment frame

Napiers were glad to help and supplied fleet mileage, availability figures and other useful information on the understanding that we covered up the origin. EE talked, but would not provide a tractive effort curve or a drawing because the source would be obvious. The manager concerned did not wish to get involved in press statements while there was the possibility of negotiations between themselves and the BRB. One longed for a George Nelson to take the Kremlin by storm again. Eastern Region were glad to help and provided up-to-date statistics on the Class 55 and "Baby Deltic" (Class 23) performance. The "Baby Deltics" were significant because they were powered by nine-cylinder versions of the turbocharged engine required for the "Super Deltic" (and by 1967 were performing very well). The ER made only one proviso—would I mind arriving at GN House after office hours and by the side door!

The result was a powerful piece in the October 1967 *Modern Railways* using the Deltic record to argue the "Super Deltic" case. The price of the new locomotives would be £150–200,000 (1967 money) with the two engines costing perhaps £40,000 more than the 4,000hp Sulzer then under development. But given spare capacity in the electrical and cooling equipment the 4,400hp of 1968 could be re-engined with the CT18-52 to make the 5,000hp Class 55 replacement of the 1970s. In fact Paxmans now reckon that the turbocharged and charge air cooled CT18-52 Deltic is the best engine of the series. But already it was too late. In the same issue of *Modern Railways* appeared the excerpts from *I Tried to Run a Railway* which removed the one man who might have got the "Super Deltic" into production. The traction engineers went back to derating Sulzers and wondering how to get more than 3,000hp into a reliable locomotive; they finally achieved this with the Class 56 in 1976.

The accompanying drawing, Fig. 3, is the official English Electric plan of the 4,400hp "Super Deltic". Everything is there as we in *Modern Railways* imagined it: two T18-27B engines, a 19 ton axle load, neatly packaged in a Class 50-type superstructure. Even today it would solve a lot of operating problems, even without the extra power of CT18-52 engines and the light weight and reliability of modern alternator transmissions and solid state control circuitry. But think what it would have meant to ER if deliveries had begun in 1967 or 1968—as much power as an HST with 20 tons less dead weight. Yet it was not a dream or a piece of journalistic wishful thinking. It was as realistic as the Class 50s which eventually met our requirement north of Crewe—working in multiple.

"Trident" "Peterborough" station on April 21, 1973.

[P. H. Wells

The Deltic bodyshell was used for the prototype No DP2 which was the forerunner of BR's 2,700 hp Class 50 diesel-electrics; No DP2 (later to be scrapped after severe damage in a collision on the ER north of York) passes Wolverton with LMR's up 'Manxman' on July 21, 1962. [*J. G. Haydon*

No 9021 *Argyll & Southern Highlander* lays a heavy trail of exhaust as it emerges from Copenhagen Tunnel, London, with the 14.00 Kings Cross–Edinburgh on April 17. 1971.

[*J. H. Cooper-Smith*

The only regular Deltic turn north of the Forth–Clyde Valley
involved a Motorail working in days when the London–Perth
service travelled the East Coast routes to and from a London
terminal at Holloway; one of the class was photographed
crossing the Forth bridge with a southbound Motorail train
on August 8, 1968. [G. P. Cooper

Deltic at Glasgow Queen Street; No 9010 *The King's Own Scottish Borderer* ready to leave with the up 'Queen of Scots' on May 26, 1962.

Unusual turn for a Deltic — No 9008, then unnamed, on the Carlisle–Newcastle line passing Brampton Junction with the summer Saturday Ayr–Newcastle train on July 29, 1961.

[*P. Brock*

Some Deltics named after Highland regiments were run
deep into Scotland for special naming ceremonies — hence
No 9019 *Royal Highland Fusilier* was seen at Aviemore on
April 15, 1969 piloting Class 26 No 5338 to Inverness with
the morning mail from Perth. [*D. Cross*

Another special naming ceremony found No 9010 *The
King's Own Scottish Borderer* at Dumfries on May 8, 1965;
it is here leaving after the ceremony with a special troop train
to Inverness carrying KOSB Territorials to their annual camp.

[*D. A. MacNaught*

Above: Deltic diverted: No 9001 passes Benton with the Sunday 10.50 Edinburgh–Kings Cross diverted via South Gosforth on April 15, 1962 because of engineering works on the main line at Heaton.   [*I. S. Carr*

Opposite, top: Another Deltic off its normal tracks ¬ No 9010 comes off the branch from Castleford at Garforth with the Sunday 10.10 Kings Cross–Leeds diverted because of engineering work at Hunslet.   [*J. M. Rayner*

Opposite, foot: Deltic on the GE line; No 9012 *Crepello* moves the empty stock on the Leeds–Bressingham railway enthusiasts' special from Diss to Stowmarket through Haughley on Sunday May 17, 1970.   [*D. R. Mortimer*

Above: Final style — renumbered 55.018, *Ballymoss* heads a train of Mark 2d air-conditioned stock out of Kings Cross on the 11.25 service to Leeds on June 12, 1973 [*Brian Morrison*

Below: Deltic on the Western — borrowed by the WR for a special London—South Wales excursion on October 12, 1975, No 55.003 *Meld* passes Severn Tunnel Junction *en route* back from Cardiff to Paddington. [*Barry J. Nicolle*

The Deltic Timetable

by BRIAN PERREN

DURING THE four-year period preceding the arrival of the 22 Deltic locomotives through to the introduction of the complete East Coast route Deltic accelerations in June 1962, the progressive build-up of the British Rail diesel fleet had shown—despite a number of technical problems with some types—the utilisation potential of the new motive power. It was, however, with the advent of the Deltic fleet that the first major breakthrough in speed, frequency, locomotive and coaching stock utilisation—in line with the aims and objectives of BR's 1954 Modernisation Plan—was achieved. Whilst it was of course true that the Deltics were built exclusively for main-line passenger work over a compact geographical area, working very fast trains in a timetable based on standard hourly departures and thus enabling them to be programmed in ideal circumstances, the daily scheduled mileages and hours in traffic planned for the 1962 timetable were a staggering advance on the standards of the steam era.

Before examining in detail the programming, utilisation and maintenance arrangements for the Deltic fleet, one should recall the train planning philosophy for the 1962 East Coast main-line timetable and subsequent developments. Target schedules in 1962 for the fastest trains were an even six hours between Kings Cross and Edinburgh, four hours between Kings Cross and Newcastle, and three hours between Kings Cross and Leeds. Exact times varied according to the number of intermediate stops. Deltic power was allocated to these services, while the remaining trains, after the final elimination of steam in 1963, were to be hauled by Brush Type 4 2,750hp locomotives now known as Class 47.

The second planning assumption was that the pattern of service would be on a standard departure basis throughout most of the day with additional trains at the business peaks. This provided the opportunity for intensive locomotive and stock utilisation based on short turn-rounds, with a regular pattern of departing trains providing opportunities for return workings. The basic system of standard time departures from Kings Cross to Newcastle and Edinburgh and for southbound departures from Edinburgh was maintained for several years. But the need of additional trains to cope with the steady annual increase in Inter-City business during the 14 or so years after the introduction of the first Deltic accelerations in 1962 gradually enforced many changes to the original Deltic timetable.

The first important deviation from the standard-time concept was made in the mid-1960s. At that time the first of a number of fast, tightly timed, limited-load trains were introduced to meet the requirements of businessmen wishing to take advantage of an early start from the North-East or the West Riding to spend a full day for business in London. Similar northbound trains were run from Kings Cross. Originally most of these "Deltic-plus-eight trains" were, of course, programmed for Deltic power, but some are now hauled by Class 47s.

During the early 1970s work started on a progressive programme of track works on the East Coast main line and the steady build-up began of long sections of route passed for 100mph running. By May 1973 no less than 211 miles, or 80 per cent, of the route between Kings Cross and Newcastle was fit for 100mph. New point-to-point running times based on the new line speed limits—but also reflecting the effects of re-equipping the Deltic fleet to supply current from the locomotive main generator for heating and air-conditioning of the new Mk II coaches—were introduced for the 1971 and 1973 time-tables, and further revisions followed in May 1975.

Faced with the prospect of a substantial deceleration of Kings Cross–Edinburgh daytime trains, necessitated by single-line working over parts of the route between Berwick and Edinburgh so that engineers could prepare for the High Speed Train, plus the need for additional recovery time in the Kings Cross area to offset the effects of electrification engineering, the ER had decided to tighten up their running times still further, by increasing the demand on the Deltics. Previously, in contrast with other BR Regions, where times were computed on 100 per cent locomotive power output, the ER had preferred to work on 85 per cent, which gave them a margin of reserve in addition to the usual recovery-time allowance. The increase began with a step to 90 per cent in 1973 and then the full 100 per cent in 1975. This implied an increase in maintenance costs, but it was the only way to minimise the extension of journey times. In 1973 the best timing between Kings Cross and Newcastle was 3hr 25min with a "Deltic-plus-eight" formation making an intermediate stop at Darlington. Today the best from Newcastle to Kings Cross by a "Deltic-plus-eight" is 3hr 36min with two stops. However, the

"Flying Scotsman" runs northbound non-stop from Kings Cross to Newcastle in 3hr 33min, compared with 4hr 1min in 1962.

As the 1962 timetable plan took shape the link-up between the new journey times and the scope for intensive utilisation was carried into the locomotive diagrams. Not only did the new journey times provide an improved public service, but the earlier arrival of the trains at their destinations made it possible for the Deltics to turn round for an earlier return working. This is basically how the 22 Deltics were able to displace 55 steam locomotives.

A further contribution to this saving followed from an early decision whereby—irrespective of Regional allocation—the fleet of Deltics would be utilised on a pooled basis. Thus, although the original fleet allocation of eight locomotives to Clarence Yard depot in the Eastern Region, six to Gateshead in the North Eastern Region and eight to Haymarket in the Scottish Region was for maintenance purposes, the planning of the work for the fleet would be inter-Regional. All Inter-City train planning for the East Coast route is on this basis. Also, day-to-day operating control of the locomotives is centralised with supervision in the Regional Control Office of the Eastern Region Movement Headquarters at York. Under centralised control it is possible to obtain full fleet flexibility.

The most important factor in programming a fleet of locomotives is finding the optimum level of day-to-day availability which can be reliably achieved throughout the year. Obviously this should not be set at a level where there is insufficient cover for important Deltic-hauled trains, nor at the other extreme where Deltics are under-employed. Based on experience over the years the right balance seems to have been found by having 17 daily diagrams for the 22 loco-motives, though in 1974/75 the effects of a spares shortage required a reduction temporarily to 15.

Servicing of the Deltic fleet was originally based on a maintenance schedule which provided for an "A" examination every 24hr, a "B" every seven working days, a "C" every 28 working days, and a "D" every 84 working days. The 1976 schedule is given on page 29. Although it is a short examination, the "A" check has no fewer than 15 separate items to be covered in the short time allowed. These include a standard visual safety check, lubricating oil levels, steam-heating boiler test, engine cooling water-level and aws. Time for an "A" examination, which normally takes about 2½hr, is provided in each individual locomotive diagram.

In many cases it is possible to utilise the normal layover time between trains for an "A" examination, and for this reason the examination is not necessarily made at the base depot. The planners select the depot location for the work at a convenient point in the diagram; a flexibility tolerance of 4hr over the standard 24hr assists diagramming. To save time at the London end of the East Coast main-line the locomotive yard at Kings Cross station is equipped to carry out "A" examinations; otherwise the locomotives would have to run out to Clarence Yard and back, necessitating a longer layover, which would reduce utilisation potential. Examinations between trips at Leeds, Newcastle, or Edinburgh are made at Holbeck, Gateshead and Haymarket, where access to the depot is easier.

Although a "B" examination takes between 8 and 12hr, it is just possible to complete this work in some of the longer layovers, particularly at weekends, when locomotive requirements are reduced. Time for "C" and "D" examinations and works visits is covered by the five undiagrammed locomotives.

To minimise the time a Deltic is in Doncaster Works, much of the maintenance is done on a unit replacement basis, so that a locomotive is not held up awaiting completion of a particular component part. There are 57 power units for the fleet, 44 for the 22 locomotives plus 13 spare for repair or replacement; six spare bogies; and 10 spare main generators. Each locomotive visits Doncaster Works for a light overhaul every 10 months, completed in about five working days, and every 20 months for an intermediate overhaul, completed in about 15 working days.

By far the most important change compared with the 1962 timetable has been the dramatic increase in the frequency of the East Coast main line service. This, together with some loss of potential availability to work with a higher margin of reserve than the level originally planned for 1962, now means that a high proportion of trains has to be worked with Class 47 diesels. Of the 35 or so daytime Inter-City departures (including those to North Humberside) from Kings Cross in the 1975/76 timetable only 13 could be rostered for Deltic haulage.

With one exception all the daytime Kings Cross–Edinburgh trains each way are Deltic-hauled. With pressure to make the best use of the available Deltic fleet a number of changes in basic programming have been made to position locomotives for commercially important return workings. Whereas previously all East Coast trains between London and Edinburgh were hauled by Deltic or Class 47 power throughout a number of changes are now made. For example, the Deltic heading the southbound 22.50 from Edinburgh is removed from this train at Newcastle so that it is in position to work the 08.20 Newcastle to Edinburgh later the same morning Similarly, as the loading of the southbound "Hull Pullman" has had to be increased to cope with the growing number of passengers a Deltic is now rostered for this train. But as it would be a waste of Deltic earning capacity to stable a locomotive overnight at Hull, the Deltic of the southbound 22.30 from Edinburgh to Kings Cross is detached at Doncaster, whence it works over to Hull.

Originally the diagrams for the Deltic fleet were all prepared on a seven-day cyclic basis. Each locomotive would follow through a sequence of trains on a weekly basis. These seven-day cycles included time both for "A" and "B" examinations. In the light of experience, however, these long cycles were found to be needlessly complicated, particularly when a locomotive was stopped for a defect or missed a scheduled turn-round, thereby breaking the cycle. Subsequently, therefore, the diagrams were broken down into groups covering shorter periods.

A further simplification was introduced in May 1970, when locomotive diagrams for the three Deltic based depots were abolished and replaced by a set of 17 diagrams for the fleet without reference to specific depots. Previously there were seven diagrams for the eight locomotives at Clarence Yard, four for the six Gateshead locomotives and six for the eight Haymarket locomotives. Although there was still a total of 17 diagrams, better use of the fleet was obtained and a spare locomotive available, say, at Gateshead could be switched into any of the 17 diagrams to cover a failure elsewhere or to replace any of the 22 Deltics away in Doncaster Works. Some of the 17 diagrams, however, were grouped into simple three-day cycles.

A five-day cycle for five Deltics in the 1975/76 timetable represents a typical programme of work. Starting service after maintenance at Clarence Yard depot the locomotive worked the 07.45 from Kings Cross to Edinburgh, due at 13.33. After a brief turnround, it returned south with the 14.50 Edinburgh to Kings Cross due at 20.37, fuelled at Kings Cross and worked the 22.45 Kings Cross to Newcastle, due at 03.24. Taking on fuel and undergoing examination at Gateshead, the Deltic started the second day with the 08.30 Newcastle to Kings Cross, followed by the 15.55 "Deltic-plus-eight" train to Leeds, due 18.26. Unusually, prior to the next Inter-City working back to Kings Cross, it then covered some empty stock working in the Leeds area and a local working to Harrogate plus the return empty stock to Neville Hill. After fuel and examination it then stabled before starting the third day with the 02.15 from Leeds to Kings Cross, due at 06.12. This was followed by the 09.00 Kings Cross to Newcastle;

15.06 Newcastle to Kings Cross, due 19.11; and the overnight 22.15 "Night Aberdonian" as far as Edinburgh, arriving at 04.47. After fuel and examination at Haymarket Depot, day four consisted of a return trip to London with the 07.55 Edinburgh to Kings Cross, due 13.38, and the 17.00 Kings Cross to Edinburgh, due 22.37. The fifth and final day of the cycle comprised three single 392.8 mile trips, starting with the southbound "Night Aberdonian" from Edinburgh at 00.30, due Kings Cross at 07.07, then taking up the 10.00 "Flying Scotsman" from Kings Cross to Edinburgh, due 15.41, and finishing with the 17.00 Edinburgh to Kings Cross due 22.39. Fuel and examination at Clarence Yard preceded a repeat of the cycle.

Because the Deltics are employed exclusively on East Coast and London–Leeds passenger trains each of the 17 daily diagrams has inevitably included at least one visit to the southern terminal of the East Coast route at Kings Cross, and accommodation and turn-round of the Deltics at Kings Cross is obviously an important factor.

Prior to the 1977 alterations and remodelling of the terminal a particular difficulty was the unsatisfactory layout at the station and the location of the small locomotive yard on a cramped site on the western side of the station. Locomotives off up trains had to per-form three separate movements—from the platform back into one of the tunnels, reversing across the connections to the suburban group of platforms, and reversing again into the locomotive yard. During the midday periods, when traffic at the station is light, these move-ments were made without difficulty, but from around 16.00 onwards, when the station handled the late afternoon Inter-City series of departures, closely followed by the suburban peak, the movement of locomotives became increasingly difficult. As each movement to or from the locomotive yard blocked platform No 14, scheduled to handle some twelve GN suburban departures from Moorgate between 16.30 and 18.30, a high degree of co-ordination was necessary between the station signalmen and the locomotive yard staff.

The fastest turnround at the time of writing involved the Deltic off the 09.45 from Edinburgh, which arrived at 15.27. It was released at 16.00, was into the depot for refuelling and inspection at 16.20, left the depot at 17.44 and then took on the 18.02 train. This gave a 1hr 24min turnround which is close to the limit. There were several others in the 2–2½hr range. In such a situation the "A" (28hr) examination is carried out at whichever depot the locomotive happens to be at at the time.

Quick turn-rounds at Kings Cross are necessary, despite the difficulties of the terminal working during the evening peak. By the early evening almost all of the 15 Deltics in daily service are actually out on the road working trains. During this period, therefore, each locomotive must have the minimum possible turn-round time if all the Deltic-manned trains are to be covered. A short scheduled turn-round has been for the locomotive arriving at 18.35 with the 12.03 from Edinburgh, which was required to work the 20.15 back to Edinburgh—a layover of 1hr 40min, but by this time in the evening conditions in the station are easier.

This peak demand for Deltic power follows the pattern of the Inter-City service. During the day, when the service comprises about two trains per hour in each direction, there is spare power. But additional trains for returning businessmen, starting with the 15.55 and followed by other Deltic-hauled trains at 16.00, 16.30, 17.00 and 1804, led up to the night period, with the 20.15 when all available Deltic locomotives have been required. Night Deltic departures followed at 22.15, 22.30, 22.45, 22.50 and 23.55, and there has been a similar series of trains in the up direction from Newcastle or Edinburgh.

Except for the 07.20 Bradford to Kings Cross and 06.45 "Hull Pullman" from Hull to Kings Cross all Deltics work within the area Kings Cross–Leeds or Kings Cross–Newcastle–Edinburgh. There used to be a regular summer exception when a Deltic worked the up Perth–Holloway Motorail train from Perth to London, but this train now operates over the London Midland mainline to Kensington.

Finally, a word on crewing arrangements for the Deltics. Gone, of course, is the steam-era practice of allocating regular crews to nominated locomotives. Crews from Kings Cross, Gateshead or Haymarket are booked to work Deltics from any of these depots regardless of allocation. Also crews from Doncaster, Holbeck and York, where there are no Deltic allocations, are programmed to work Deltic-hauled trains.

The most important change in the diesel era is the new pattern of drivers' work following the substantial accelerations and reduced journey times. Now that the average journey between Kings Cross and Leeds is well under three hours, duties covering return trips between these points in a normal shift can be planned on an extensive basis. There are also some similar turns between York and Kings Cross. All lodging turns between Kings Cross, Leeds or York have been discontinued. There are also, however, the long non-stop runs still operative between Kings Cross and Darlington or Newcastle— actually the longest in Great Britain today—and these, all Deltic-hauled, require their Kings Cross or Gateshead crews to lodge away.

But the lot of their drivers has improved out of all recognition. Instead of spending about 1¼hr at Gateshead Depot preparing a Pacific to take over the up "Flying Scotsman" for the non-stop 5hr run to Kings Cross, a driver now reports to Newcastle Central shortly before departure and relieves the incoming crew during the 3min stop.

Deltic Performance

by CECIL J. ALLEN

Publisher's Note: *This chapter, "Deltic Performance", was written by the late Cecil J. Allen in 1970, since when there has been a great and progressive improvement in express train schedules on the East Coast main line and into the industrial centres of West Yorkshire. This has been made possible not only by the intensive diagramming of the Deltic fleet—with sterling support by the less powerful Brush "Type 4s" of Class 47, but most notably in recent years, by the huge programme of re-alignments and track improvement. In order to bring this chapter more closely into line with current standards of train running, it has been sympathetically revised and up-dated by D. S. M. Barrie, who was not only a friend and admirer of "C.J.A.", but also collaborated with him on some notable record steam-hauled journeys in the 1930s. Moreover, as an Assistant General Manager and finally General Manager of the Eastern Region, Mr Barrie was closely associated with the acceleration of East Coast services between 1961–70.*

The early parts of this chapter are, with some minor interpolations, as C.J.A. wrote them. But elsewhere substantial changes have been made, and in some cases the tabulated logs have been rearranged, or condensed to reduce the amount of intermediate detail rendered scarcely necessary by virtue of the elimination or easement of hitherto intervening speed restrictions.

AT THE END of 1955 the prototype Deltic was completed, and in 1956 it was loaned by English Electric to British Railways for exhaustive testing before delivery began in 1961 of the 22 units which were to work over the Eastern, North-Eastern and Scottish Regions. The first systematic tests, however, were made on the London Midland Region, and they were described in detail in the British Transport Commission's *Performance and Efficiency Test Bulletin No 19*—one of a series of such bulletins which previously had dealt with the performance of various types of steam locomotives. These tests were made in the summer of 1956, but actually Test Bulletin No 19 was not released for publication until two years later.

The location of the principal tests was the former Midland main-line between Skipton and Carlisle, chosen because of the opportunity it offered for maximum power output up the lengthy 1 in 100 approaches to the 1,167ft summit at Ais Gill. For the first tests the dynamometer car was attached to two of the BR Mobile Test Units, the latter to provide for exact control of the road speeds; later tests were with a train of 20 coaches (dynamometer car included), having a tare weight of 642 tons. The majority of the trials were conducted with both engines of the Deltic in action; but with the help of the change-over switches that make it possible to drive all six motors from one power unit, other tests were with one engine only. In the latter case the same tractive effort can be obtained as with both engines, but at a reduced speed.

The range of power output was investigated by conducting tests at eight different settings of the controller, corresponding (with two engines in action) to engine speeds of 700, 800, 900, 1,050, 1,200, 1,300, 1,400 and 1,500rpm. With one engine only in action the tests were at 800, 900, 1,200 and 1,500rpm only. The lowest of these settings was selected in order to give the tractive power available at the idling speed, while the highest corresponded to the maximum power of the engines.

The first 15 to 20min of each run were devoted to warming up, and the engine rpm were then set by the use of the driver's controller to the required value; at each fixed setting the engine rpm, fuel consumption and bhp remained approximately constant. The Mobile Test Units were then used to control the road speed in increments of 5mph at a time, each step in speed lasting from 5 to 10min. In the dynamometer car continuous records were kept of speed, drawbar tractive effort and horsepower, together with fuel consumption in 1/5gal increments, and also electrical and diesel engine data, and cooling water and lubricating oil temperatures.

The many curves reproduced in Test Bulletin No 19 show that in the tests the performance approximated closely to the design characteristics of the Deltic. A maximum drawbar pull of 44,000lb was shown to be available at speeds up to 20mph with the engines developing a total of 3,250hp (as compared with the rated 3,300hp), and a maximum pull of 45,550lb was sustained for 2min without any slipping. At 80mph under full load the drawbar pull was 10,800lb, representing a drawbar hp of 2,300hp, or 71 per cent of the actual bhp that was being developed. The various curves showed that the drawbar hp rose almost in a straight line as the engine output advanced, from 490 drawbar hp at 24mph with an engine bhp of 696 to 2,580 drawbar hp at 42mph with engine output at the full 3,250bhp.

Under full load, and at the point of optimum power output at 42mph, the efficiency through the electric transmission, including the gearing, was shown to be almost 86 per cent, and at 80mph as high as 84 per cent. At roughly one-half and two-thirds full load the transmission efficiency also was about 84 per cent at 40mph; it is between these two ranges that the average demand on Deltic power in normal service would generally lie. Power absorption by auxiliaries was between 150 and 160hp, and fuel consumption at between 10 and 70mph averaged 600lb an hour.

With the 642-ton test train the drawbar pulls, as might be expected, did not reach quite such high values as those with the mobile test units, but up the lengthy 1 in 100 inclines to Ais Gill drawbar hps of 2,200 to 2,300 were recorded continuously at speeds of from 45 to 55mph. The southbound run was started from Durran Hill sidings, just south of Carlisle, and from the start the Deltic had to accelerate up a gradient of 1 in 133; on this a speed of 46mph was reached. A slight easing of the grade past Cumwhinton allowed an acceleration to 54mph, which was maintained up the 1 in 129 to Low House. There was then a rapid acceleration to 70mph down the short descent to Armathwaite, and the 1 in 220 to milepost 294¾ was surmounted with no greater drop in speed than from 72 to 68mph.

The main test of strength, however, was not until after the train had passed Appleby. From Ormside there is a continuous climb of 17½ miles, almost entirely at 1 in 100 save for 2 miles at 1 in 162–215 from Griseburn to Crosby Garrett and a level mile beyond, and, later, the level mile past Mallerstang box. This climb was begun at 72mph, and in the first 3½ miles at 1 in 100 speed fell to 57mph; the easier stretch past Crosby Garrett then permitted a recovery to 63 mph, while on the long final 1 in 100 speed settled down to 48–47 mph, broken only by a brief recovery to 54mph past Mallerstang.

The 47 miles from the start at Durran Hill to Ais Gill, including a 15mph permanent way slowing at Lazonby, and another to 25mph at Long Marton, had been covered in 56min. For most of the distance the drawbar hp had varied between 2,000 and 2,400, and the drawbar pull had ranged between 5 and 5½ tons on the easier stretches and 8 tons on the final 1 in 100 to Ais Gill Summit. With one engine only in operation the maximum drawbar hp varied between 1,100 at 60mph and 1,270 at 25mph; this was less than half the output with both engines working, because the power absorbed by engine resistance and auxiliaries had to be set against the output of one engine only instead of two.

Based on the tests, it was calculated that the Deltic, under full power, could work a 500-ton train up a continuous 1 in 100 at 50mph and up 1 in 75 at 41mph; up 1 in 400 with this load the top test speed of 80mph could be maintained. With a light nine-coach load of 300 tons 58mph could be sustained up 1 in 75 and 80mph up 1 in 150. With the 11-coach and 12-coach trains currently operating on the East Coast main-line schedules of 1956, having a weight of 400 tons or so, far less than the full power of the Deltic would be needed for timekeeping. As to fuel consumption, over the 165 miles of the test journeys, including the two climbs to Ais Gill Summit, with speed averaging 56.2mph, the total fuel oil consumption was 210gal, which worked out at an average of no more than 0.8gal per mile.

The Deltic storage capacity of 800gal thus would provide for a total of 630 miles of running without replenishment, but as the gradients over which the Deltics were to operate in normal service were nothing like as severe as those up to Ais Gill Summit, nor the loads anywhere near 642 tons, this fuel tank capacity should be amply sufficient for a 786-mile journey from Kings Cross to Edinburgh and back. Bulletin No 19 commented favourably on the exceptionally smooth riding and freedom from vibration of the Deltic; the only criticism was of the noisiness of the engines when idling, which might prove troublesome when standing in stations. In all, these tests of the prototype Deltic were regarded as highly successful.

During 1957 and 1958 the prototype Deltic went into London Midland revenue service, mainly between Euston and Liverpool turn-and-turn about with Stanier steam Pacifics of the "Duchess" class. A train frequently worked was the 07.55 from Euston, a heavy express which at that time had one of the fastest schedules on the LMR, from Watford Junction to Crewe, 140.55 miles in 136min. From the gradient point of view this is an exceptionally easy route, with no inclinations steeper than 1 in 330 except for the 1 in 70–105 up out of Euston and the 1 in 177–269 for 6½ miles from Madeley, the latter in favour of down trains. The only permanent speed restrictions were 40mph past Rugby and 50mph round the Trent Valley curve at Stafford (both of which have been raised to 60mph since the electrification).

The prototype Deltic had no difficulty in cutting the 136min schedule to net times of 123–124min with loads up to 15 coaches of 488 tons tare and 515 tons gross. Table 1 sets out the details of a run timed by H. A. B. Lee with a 13-coach load of 414/445 tons which was in the nature of a speed test, with speeds up to 90mph and an unscheduled stop of 9¾min at Rugby for examination, notwithstanding which, time was more than easily kept to Crewe. Indeed, without

Table I (Run No I)
LMR WATFORD JUNCTION—CREWE

Locomotive: Prototype English Electric Co-Co Deltic (3,300hp)
Load: 13 coaches, 414 tons tare, 445 tons gross

Dist		Sched	Actual		Speeds¶
miles		*min*	*min*	*sec*	*mph*
0.00	WATFORD JUNC	0	§0	00	—
14.20	TRING	16	13	45	62.0
22.75	Leighton	—	19	50	84.3
29.20	BLETCHLEY	28	24	30	84.2
34.95	Wolverton	—	28	40	82.8
42.45	*Roade*	39	34	10	82.7
45.40	*Blisworth*	42	36	20	81.7
52.25	*Weedon*	48	41	35	78.3
57.85	*Welton*	—	46	05	74.7
			sigs		*
65.10	RUGBY	†60	‡53	25	59.3
0.00	RUGBY	†0	§0	00	—
8.85	*Shilton*	—	9	00	59.0
14.55	NUNEATON	14	13	15	78.1
					*
19.75	Atherstone	—	17	30	73.5
			pws		*
23.95	Polesworth	—	21	40	60.4
27.45	TAMWORTH	27	24	15	81.3
33.70	LICHFIELD	33	28	45	82.0
38.45	*Armitage*	—	32	15	81.4
41.75	Rugeley	40	34	45	79.2
					*
44.60	*Colwich*	—	37	10	70.7
47.00	*Milford*	45	39	20	66.7
					*
51.00	STAFFORD	50	43	05	64.0
56.30	Norton Bridge	56	48	15	61.5
60.85	*Standon Bridge*	—	52	00	72.8
65.10	Whitmore	65	55	20	76.5
67.50	*Madeley*	—	57	15	75.2
70.70	*Betley Road*	—	59	45	76.8
			sigs		*
75.45	CREWE	76	67	25	—

* Speed restriction † Passing time
‡ To stop § From start ¶ Average speeds, station to station

the Rugby stop the net time would have been 116½min, or just under 20min less than that scheduled, and though a "Duchess" steam 4–6–2 could probably have equalled such a performance if driven hard, it would certainly have been regarded as exceptional for a locomotive of the latter type. Even so, in view of the different conditions prevailing before and after full electrification, close comparison between the two systems could not be afforded.

The Deltic was then transferred to the Eastern Region, and tests in 1959 soon demonstrated a tractive capacity far exceeding that required on the London Midland Region runs just described. On one run, with a 10-coach train of 355 tons tare and 350 tons gross, experiments were made to ascertain the distance needed to bring the train to rest from high speeds in an emergency. On the down journey the first such stop was made on the 1 in 200 rising grade past New Southgate; 36.2sec and a distance of 2,020ft were needed to come to a stand from a speed of 62½mph.

After passing Werrington Junction, Peterborough, at 53mph the controller was moved to full, with the result that in 2½ miles of level track there was an acceleration to 78mph, increased to 86½mph up the slight rise to Tallington; the latter speed was maintained up the 1 in 440–264 to Essendine. The next two level miles produced 92mph by milepost 91, and the 4½ miles at 1 in 200 from there were surmounted at a minimum of 88mph. Then followed a brief 92mph on the short level past Corby Glen, and a lowest rate of 86½mph up the final 3 miles at 1 in 178 to Stoke Summit. Up to that date such hill-climbing figures were unprecedented, though today they are often beaten in day-to-day running.

On the up journey on the same day a planned emergency stop from 100mph was made on the long descent southwards from Stoke. On the 1 in 200 up to Stoke a brake test was first made from 64mph, with a similar result to that at New Southgate, to a dead stand in 34.8sec and 2,010ft. The recovery of speed from Stoke Summit was cut short by a 25mph slack for track relaying just short of Corby Glen, after which there was a very rapid acceleration to 79, 85½, 92 and 97mph at the end of successive miles down 1 in 200; 100mph was reached at milepost 90¾, a gain from 68 to 100mph in 4½ miles all told. The 100mph was then held on the practically level 2 miles to Essendine, and there was next a further increase to 105mph on the subsequent 1 in 264. On passing the up distant signal for Lolham box, there came the most important brake test of all, and this time it was a considerably more lengthy business, needing a total of 72.9sec and 6,219ft to come down from 102½mph to zero—incidentally, well beyond the Lolham stop signals.

Actually the first application of the brakes in all these tests was made at the moment of passing the distant signal of the box concerned; had the brake application in this last test been made when the distant was first sighted, along this open stretch of line, on a clear dry day, the train could probably have been stopped just short of the Lolham home signal. But these stops were with the vacuum brake, and made it pretty clear that as soon as accelerated train services made 100mph speeds necessary for timekeeping, more effective braking would be needed. It is mainly for this reason that air brakes have now replaced the vacuum brake on the fastest British train services.

The test results achieved with the prototype Deltic being regarded as satisfactory, delivery of the 22 units ordered began in the early part of 1961; eventually eight of them were attached to Finsbury Park depot, Eastern Region; six to Gateshead, North Eastern Region; and eight to Haymarket, Edinburgh, Scottish Region. No 9001 figured in a test run in 1961, with a heavier 11-coach load of 373 tons tare and 380 tons gross, planned to examine the scale of passenger service acceleration which would be possible with the new motive power. The run was made from Kings Cross to Doncaster; 130min, including a total of 8min recovery time, were allowed for the 155.95 miles. This was not quite the fastest time that had ever previously been scheduled; before World War II the streamlined steam-hauled "Coronation" was booked to pass Doncaster in 128½min, but with a maximum tare load of 312 tons as compared with 373 tons, and with no restriction of speed over various sections of the line on which such limits had been imposed in the interim.

No 9001 actually made the run in 125min 8sec start to stop, but the net time, allowing for certain out-of-course delays, was 117min, or well inside the net 122min allowance. Hill-climbing achievements of note were the acceleration from 65 to 75mph up the 7¾ miles at 1 in 200 from Wood Green to Potters Bar, and the continuous 88 to 83mph up to milepost 95½, with a slight drop from 85 to 83mph up the final 1 in 178 to Stoke. Maximum speeds of 100mph and a little over were reached at various points on the journey.

With all the 22 Deltics in service, and with the support of less-powerful types embracing Classes 40 (2,000hp), 46 (2,500hp) and 47 (2,750hp), the first full diesel timetable was introduced on the East Coast main line in June 1962, the star turn being the reduction of the "Flying Scotsman's" London–Edinburgh schedule by one hour, to six hours for the 392.7 miles. It had already been fully realised, however, that in spite of the immediate benefits of this great step forward in tractive power, it was only a partial step in the pattern of express service as a whole, so long as giant locomotives, capable for instance of approaching Peterborough at 100mph had to thread their tortuous way through that ancient layout at 20mph (or Durham at 30mph) and then expend their energy in regaining speed beyond. In order to maximise the new speed capability and commercially to counter motorway and air competition, a comprehensive programme was therefore launched—which by 1980 will have involved the expenditure of £60m in a decade—involving major re-alignments (e.g. Offord, Peterborough, Durham); the raising of numerous individual restrictions; track relaying; removal of redundant connections; more advanced colour-light signalling affording better speed control and longer braking distances; and the elimination of many manual boxes and road level crossings.

Without going into excessive detail, the effect of this programme is strikingly shown in the official Eastern Region diagram, Fig. 4, on page 71. The speed bands on the right of this diagram indicate (A) line speeds (1969) before the completion of Stage 1 of these major works, (B) permissible speeds as at May 1973, and (C) speeds which would be obtainable when the High Speed Diesel Trains displaced the Deltics from the fastest services in 1978. Because Deltics are restricted to 100mph maximum service speed, trains hauled by them would only benefit marginally from the easement of restrictions specifically for the HST. The HST was to be scheduled between London and Edinburgh in 4½hr, compared with the Deltic's 5½hr, but, be that as it may, with Deltic traction and with 100mph running already in operation over 241 out of 268.3 miles between King's Cross and Newcastle, Deltic traction had already cut the best journey times of principal services to:

	Miles	Min	Average journey speed, mph
Kings Cross–Leeds	185.8	150	74.2
Kings Cross–Newcastle	268.3	212	75.9
Kings Cross–Edinburgh	392.7	330	71.2

The progressive improvement in running times obtained from the acceleration programme is shown in great detail in the following Table 2, specially prepared for this edition by Gordon Pettitt. These depict the point-to-point running times (Kings Cross start to passing Doncaster in all cases), for each of the more critical years concerned, and for the two principal Deltic loading schedules, 280 tons and 385 tons respectively—although in actual working, these loads are often exceeded and booked time maintained. From 1970 onwards an allowance was made for electric train heating and air-conditioning requirements, and timings were based on 85 per cent power output, raised to 90 per cent from 1973, and 100 per cent from 1975. This brings us to a point stressed at some length by Cecil J. Allen in the

Table 2
DELTIC RUNNING TIME IMPROVEMENTS 1961–75
(Point-to-point timings in minutes)

385 ton trains

	1961	*1966*	*1970*	*1973*	*1975*
Kings Cross–Potters Bar	14½	14	14	14½	14
Potters Bar–Hatfield	4½	4	4½	3½	} 12½
Hatfield–Hitchin	11½	10½	10½	9½	
Hitchin–Huntingdon	19½	18	17	—17	16½
Huntingdon–Peterborough	15½	14½	13½	11½	11
Total Kings Cross–Peterborough	65½	61	59½	56	54
Peterborough–Essendine	11½	11	11½	8	} 16
Essendine–Stoke	8	8	9½	9	
Stoke–Grantham	4	4	4	4	3½
Total Peterborough–Grantham	23½	23	25	21	19½
Grantham–Newark	10½	10½	9½	9	9
Newark–Retford	15	14	13	13	13
Retford–Doncaster	15	15	13	13	13
Total Grantham–Doncaster	40½	39½	35½	35	35
Total Kings Cross–Doncaster	129½	123½	120	112	108½
RECOVERY ADDED	14	10	9	11	12

280 ton trains (250 tons in 1966)

		1966	1970	1973	1975
Kings Cross–Potters Bar	Introduced April 1966	13½	13½	13	13
Potters Bar–Hatfield		4	4	3½	} 11½
Hatfield–Hitchin		10	9½	8½	
Hitchin–Huntingdon		17½	16½	16½	16½
Huntingdon–Peterborough		14	13	11	10½
Total Kings Cross–Peterborough		59	56½	52½	51½
Peterborough–Essendine		10½	10½	7½	} 15
Essendine–Stoke		7½	8½	7½	
Stoke–Grantham		4	3½	3½	3½
Total Peterborough–Grantham		22	22½	18½	18½
Grantham–Newark		10	8½	9	9
Newark–Retford		14	12	12½	12½
Retford–Doncaster		16	13½	12½	12½
Total Grantham–Doncaster		40	34	34	34
Total Kings Cross–Doncaster		121	113	105	104
RECOVERY ADDED		5	6	8	12

Note: All timings start Kings Cross and pass Doncaster. All timings net of recovery allowances. Timings from 1970 include electric train heating allowance. Timings from 1975 based on 100 per cent output compared with 85 per cent from 1970 (90 per cent from 1973). This has narrowed the gap between 280–385 ton trains. Also air-conditioning.

first edition of this book. A basic feature of most high-power loco-motives is inability to use full horsepower at low speeds, and in early days of their work this was often a marked characteristic of the Deltics, especially when starting up-grade, such as from Kings Cross, or from Berwick-on-Tweed up the 1 in 190 to Burnmouth. Two factors have served to ameliorate this tendency. As described in a previous chapter, an ETH modification carried out in 1971 involves most of the load being taken in the initial stages by the leading generator, and there is more sensitive control of power at starting. Secondly, with meticulous training and wider experience, driving expertise is obviously greater; but while the elimination or easement of so many speed restrictions might appear to make the driver's task easier, the writer knows from footplate experience that it takes real artistry to keep the needle dead on the 100 mark for miles on end over frequent, if usually slight, changes in gradient. This point is clearly brought out in some of the tabulated runs which now follow.

However, some striking exuberance was recorded by Cecil J. Allen on a special run staged in 1967 in order to test the riding character-istics at speed of new Mk IIA coaches. It was made from Newcastle to Kings Cross, but as various delays were experienced over other stages the tabulation is confined to the two fastest stretches. As will be seen from Table 3 (Run No 2) an average of 100.4mph was maintained for a total of 52.25 miles, with maxima of 110mph at the foot of 4½ miles at 1 in 200, near Little Bytham, and of 108mph at Tempsford, after a very short descent at 1 in 330; from Tempsford to Sandy an average of 106.7mph was maintained on the level and up 1 in 264. Note should be taken also of the average of 94.1mph up the continuous 1 in 200 from Hitchin to Stevenage (old station). This was with the eight-coach load of the high-speed services.

Turning now to examples of Deltic running in ordinary service, the runs which follow are generally of a more recent vintage than those tabulated in the first edition, although some of the latter are included to afford comparison with earlier speed restrictions now eased or abolished. Table 4, in which Runs 3 and 4 were recorded by Gordon Pettitt, depict performance with loads of 279, 400 and 466 tons respectively, all between Kings Cross and Doncaster. Run No 4, on the 3.55pm high-speed business service to Leeds, suffered no greater hindrance than two pw slacks, albeit the first was practically at the foot of the climb to Stoke Summit. With careful attention to line speeds, this driver averaged 90.2mph over the 146.4 miles Wood Green–Rossington (both checks included), 97.1mph for 74.5 miles Wood Green–Werrington, and precisely 100mph over the 56 miles

Table 3 (Run No 2)
ER TEST RUN WITH MARK IIA COACHES

Locomotive: Type 55 Co-Co Diesel No 9016
Load: 8 coaches, 279 tons tare, 290 tons gross
FASTEST STRETCHES OF UP JOURNEY

Dist		Times		*Speed
miles		min	sec	mph
0.00	Stoke	0	00	pass
3.00	Corby Glen	2	08	84.4
7.85	Little Bytham	4	52	106.5
11.45	Essendine	6	52	108.0
15.25	Tallington	8	59	107.7
18.20	Helpston	10	47	99.3
20.60	Werrington Junc	12	40	†76.5

Corby Glen to Helpston, 15.20 miles in 8min 39sec = 105.8mph
Maximum speed, Little Bytham, 110.0mph

0.00	St Neots	0	00	pass
4.25	Tempsford	2	35	98.7
7.60	Sandy	4	28	106.7
10.60	Biggleswade	6	11	104.5
14.65	Arlesey	8	34	102.0
16.05	Three Counties	9	22	105.0
19.85	HITCHIN	11	34	103.6
23.20	Stevenage	13	40	94.1
26.70	Knebworth	15	52	95.4
28.25	Woolmer Green	16	48	93.2
29.75	Welwyn North	17	48	90.0
31.45	Welwyn Garden City	18	49	100.3
34.05	HATFIELD	20	29	‡93.6

Tempsford to Hitchin, 15.60 miles in 8min 59sec = 101.1mph
Maximum speed, Tempsford, 108.0mph

Notes: *Average, station to station †Speed reduced to 66mph ‡Speed reduced to 80mph
Total distance covered at 100.4mph average, 52.25 miles (Stoke–Helpston and St Neots–Hatfield)

between Woolmer Green–Werrington. Although not tabulated, D. S. M. Barrie recorded a run on the same train somewhat earlier, with No 9020 hauling 312/325 tons; Doncaster was passed in 109¾ min. The most striking feature of No 9020's journey was an acceleration from 96mph through Huntingdon to 99mph at Leys (MP 62) up 1 in 200; the only delays were moderate signal checks at Connington and approaching Doncaster, and a slack to 40mph over the new alignment at Peterborough, not then ready for 100mph running.

Table 4 (Runs 3, 4, 5)
ER KINGS CROSS–DONCASTER

Date: *Locomotive:* Type 55 Co-Co
Diesel No
Load: Coaches/tons/tare/gross

		(Feb 1974) 55 007 8/279/295			(March 1973) 9009 11/400/420			— 9007 13/466/490		
Dist		**Sched**	**Actual**	**Speeds**	**Sched**	**Actual**	**Speeds**	**Sched**	**Actual**	**Speeds**
miles		min	min sec	mph	min	min sec	mph	min	min sec	mph
0.00	KINGS CROSS	0	0 00	—	0	0 00	—	0	0 00	—
2.50	Finsbury Park	—	4 55	60	—	5 28	52/60*	—	5 08	—
4.95	Wood Green	—	7 07	75	—	7 53	63	—	7 30	65
12.70	Potters Bar	13	12 43	88	14	14 43	70	15	14 11	72
17.70	HATFIELD	18	15 57	94/87	18	18 30	82/64*	19	sigs 18 15	*63 75/86
23.50	Woolmer Green	(†2)	19 45	90/88	(†2)	pws 25 37	*30	—	pws 23 03	*58
27.60	Stevenage (New)	—	22 18	100	—	—	68	—	—	72
31.90	HITCHIN	27	24 53	100	31	31 28	88	30	29 03	90
41.15	Biggleswade	36	30 20	99/101	39	36 58	101/98	38	eased 35 02	90/100
44.15	Sandy	—	32 05	100	—	38 43	98	—	36 49	*82
51.75	St Neots	—	36 39	101	—	43 13	101/98	—	41 20	100
58.85	HUNTINGDON	45	40 52	101	48	47 32	102	48½	46 33	102
62.00	Milepost 62	—	42 45	98	—	49 27	94	—	48 52	100/*68
69.35	Holme	(†2)	47 07	100	(†3)	53 55	100	(†3)	54 00	82
75.00	Fletton Junc	—	50 30	99	—	57 47 pws	88/*64 *40	—	58 43	82 90/*75 *50

		58	51 20	100	65	59 36	*40	67½	61 58	stop
76.35	PETERBOROUGH	—		101	—		74			—
79.50	Werrington Junc		53 09 pws			62 50		5	6 37	
84.85	Tallington	66	57 25	30	76	66 51	86	—	10 50	85
88.65	Essendine		61 22	80		69 26	90	12½	13 26	90
92.25	Little Bytham		63 45	88		71 51	86	—	15 49	92
97.10	Corby Glen		66 57	96	85	75 16	85	—	19 06	88/90
100.10	Stoke	73	68 52	91	89	77 25	80	21	21 09	87/*75
105.45	GRANTHAM	77	72 15	98		80 58	91	25	25 04	90/*72
109.70	Barkston South Junc	79	74 47	100		83 38	100	28½	28 11	96
120.10	NEWARK	86	81 13 pws	100/80* 98/30*	98	eased 90 36	*77	35½	34 33	102/*80 *69
127.45	Crow Park	—	—	—	—	95 47	91	—	—	85
131.90	Tuxford	—	91 30	76	112	98 46	87	—	40 21	77
138.60	RETFORD	98	96 07	91/80*		103 27	91/*76 84/*30	50	48 47	*60
143.95	Ranskill		99 35	100	(†3)	sigs 107 58	—	—	eased 53 24	—
147.70	Bawtry	(†2)	102 00	*82		111 30	75	(†4)	56 41	—
151.35	Rossington		104 32	92		114 16	82	—	60 07	—
153.20	Black Carr Junc	—	105 44	*80		sigs	*47	—	61 47	—
156.00	DONCASTER	‡113	108 33	*40	129	119 00	*30	70½	66 24	stop
			(to Leeds) 103			(to York) 113				
	Net time (mins)							60½	70½	

* Speed restriction † Recovery time (min) ‡ Passing time

Run No 4 is a representative good performance by the "Tees–Tyne Pullman" (alas, now sadly defunct) with its normal load of 400 tons or so. After the initial pw slowing for re-alignment works near Hatfield, there was a clear road to Retford except for the same 40mph slack over the new alignment at Peterborough; even so, the 106.7 miles Hitchin–Retford were reeled off in 72 min, average 88.9mph, while an average of 98.6mph was achieved for 37½ miles between Hitchin and Holme with no greater excess than 1mph over the authorised maximum. Even with such running as this the ultimate capacity of Deltics with 400ton loads was not required, since from Grantham, with time in hand, the driver eased to avoid delays from the preceding semi-fast, whose signals were nevertheless encountered from Ranskill onwards. The continuation of this journey from passing Doncaster is not tabulated, but in spite of a brief signal stop and a pw check between Templehirst and Selby, and with a maximum of 94mph near Naburn, the 188.2 miles from London to York were completed in 151½min, a gain of 5½min on schedule. Kings Cross had been left 2min late, so the arrival was 3½min early.

As an interpolation in regard to this Doncaster–York section, Mr Pettitt recorded a remarkable sprint by the 6pm (Saturdays) Kings Cross–Newcastle train, then scheduled to cover the 32.20 miles concerned in 29min start-to-stop; the load comprised 11 vehicles, 376/395 tons and the Deltic at its head was then No 9005. In a lightning start, 70mph was attained in 2 miles, 85mph in 4¼ miles (Shaftholme Junction), and the 100mph mark was reached at Heck, in 11 miles of virtually level going. This speed was sustained until slacking to 62 through Selby, after which 96mph was regained at Naburn, 28.10 miles from the start in 21min. With a slack to 55mph over Chaloner Whin Junction, and the usual cautious entry into Platform 14, the train stopped at York in 26min 18sec for the 32.20 miles, a start-to-stop average of 73.5mph.

Reverting to Table 4, Run No 5 involved a 13 coach train of nearly 500 tons gross, and took place before the easement of speed restrictions round the Offord curves, across the fen between Holme and Yaxley, and, on the Peterborough–Doncaster stage, at Newark, Trent, and between Retford and Doncaster. This journey was recorded by the late Mr Allen, who wrote:

"Once again the climbing was notable. We maintained 82mph up the 1 in 200 from Huntingdon to milepost 62; the acceleration from 85 to 90mph between Tallington and Essendine was partly up 1 in 264; at the top of the 4½ miles at 1 in 200 before Corby Glen the speed was 87mph; and after a recovery to 89 on the short level past

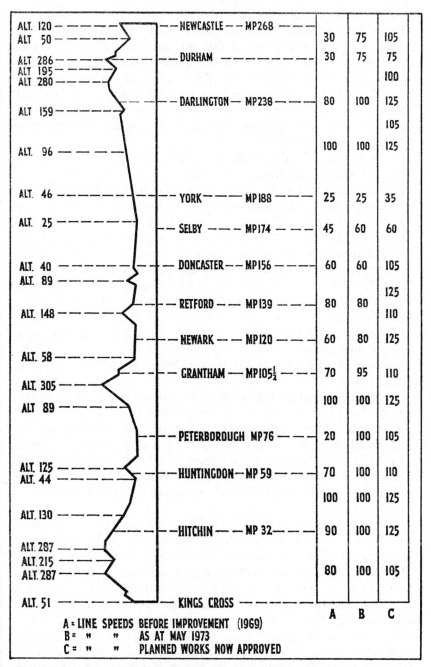

	A	B	C
ALT. 120 — — — — — NEWCASTLE — MP268 — — —			
ALT. 50 — — — — —	30	75	105
ALT. 286 — — — — DURHAM — — — — — —	30	75	75
ALT. 195 — — — —			100
ALT. 280 — — — —			
ALT. 159 — — — — — DARLINGTON — MP238 — — —	80	100	125
			105
ALT. 96 — — — —	100	100	125
ALT. 46 — — — — — — — YORK — — — MP188 — — —	25	25	35
ALT. 25 — — — — — — — SELBY — — — MP174 — — —	45	60	60
ALT. 40 — — — — — — — DONCASTER — — MP156 — — —	60	60	105
ALT. 89 — — — — —			125
ALT. 148 — — — — — RETFORD — — MP139 — — —	80	80	110
ALT. 58 — — — — — NEWARK — — MP120 — — —	60	80	125
ALT. 305 — — — — GRANTHAM — MP105½ — — —	70	95	110
ALT 89 — — — —	100	100	125
— — — PETERBOROUGH MP76 — — —	20	100	105
ALT. 125 — — — — — HUNTINGDON — MP 59 — — —	70	100	110
ALT. 44 — — — —	100	100	125
ALT. 130 — — — —			
— — — HITCHIN — — MP 32 — — —	90	100	125
ALT. 287 — —			
ALT. 215 — — —	80	100	105
ALT. 287 — —			
ALT. 51 — — — — — KINGS CROSS — — — — —	A	B	C

A = LINE SPEEDS BEFORE IMPROVEMENT (1969)
B = "   "   AS AT MAY 1973
C = "   "   PLANNED WORKS NOW APPROVED

Fig. 4.   Kings Cross to Newcastle; Distance, Gradients and Line Speeds.

Corby, the final 3 miles at 1 in 178 were carried at a minimum of 87mph. The controller must have been at full continuously for such a feat as this. It will be noted that no more than 27min 7sec was taken to run the 40.8 miles from Stevenage to Holme, at an average speed of precisely 90mph. So Peterborough was reached in 61min 58sec from Kings Cross, or 60½min net—the latter a gain of 7min on schedule—and beyond Retford on the second stage No 9007 had to be eased to avoid gaining too much time, though even so there was a further gain of 3min here."

As examples of running in the reverse (Up) direction between York, Doncaster and Kings Cross, three runs (Nos 6, 7 and 8) have been selected so as to demonstrate the effect of the raising of key speed restrictions, while still depicting first-class Deltic performance. Run No 6, recorded by Mr Pettitt on the 4pm from Edinburgh when both the slack over Selby swing-bridge and the devious crawl through the old Peterborough station were still in force, and when Hitchin rather than (New) Stevenage was still the setting-down stop for Outer London, was a noteworthy effort whereby a 15min late start from York was converted into a 2min early arrival. The 156.25 miles from York to Hitchin were run at an average start-to-stop speed of 81.3mph, or in the identical net time then allowed a Deltic hauling a train of only 280 tons, and this with all speed limits observed; it was equivalent to a net time of 138min for the 188¼ miles from York to Kings Cross.

The value of raising the Selby restriction is clearly shown in the run by No 55 001 on the "Tees–Tyne Pullman" in the top half of the second column; with similar speeds by both trains at Riccall and Shaftholme, No 55 001 by traversing Selby at 59mph gained about 1½min on the non-stopping train, and despite the usual careful crawl into the east side of the up island platform at Doncaster, stopped there in less time than it took the non-stopping train to pass on the through road.

Run No 8, in the lower half of the second column, also features the "Tees–Tyne Pullman", with load reduced by one coach, on an occasion when it was stopped momentarily in Newark station. Despite an excellent initial climb out of the Trent Valley, whereby parity in speed with the Edinburgh train had almost been attained by Grantham, the Pullman took over 4min more to pass Stoke summit than No 9006 took pass-to-pass: a striking indication of the extra cost of a signal stop with motive power of this capacity. The Pullman was also slightly slower down the ensuing bank, but with the advantage of full speed over the Peterborough new alignment and

Table 5 *(Runs 6, 7, 8)*
ER YORK–DONCASTER–KINGS CROSS

Locomotive: Type 55 Co-Co Diesel No Load: coaches/tons tare/gross		9006 12/400/420			55 001 11/395/410			
Dist		Sched	Actual	Speeds	Sched	Actual	Speeds	
miles		min	min sec	mph	min	min sec	mph	
0.00	YORK	—	0 00	—	—	0 00	—	
2.00	Chaloner _Whin Junc	—	3 48	*55	—	3 26	*52	
4.10	Naburn	—	5 50	74	—	5 34	70	
9.65	Riccall	—	9 47	95	—	9 23	93	
13.90	SELBY	15	13 25	*45	13½	12 23	*59	
18.40	Templehirst	—	17 32	80	—	15 58	85	
22.25	Balne	†3	20 10	94	—	—	95	
28.15	Shaftholme Junc	29	23 40	98/*88	23½	21 52	100	
30.10	Arksey	—	25 15	*80	—	—	*79	
32.20	DONCASTER	33	27 10	*57	28	26 57 stop	—	
36.80	Rossington	—	31 15	77				
40.45	Bawtry	—	33 53	*80	Locomotive: 55 003			
49.55	RETFORD	47	40 02	91/*80	Load: 10/357/370 tons			Dist
54.20	Milepost 134	—	43 24	77	(Restart from sig stop			from
56.90	Tuxford	—	44 50	87	at Newark)			Newark
60.70	Crow Park	—	47 33	100				
—	Carlton	—	sigs	*77	Sched	min sec	mph	miles
68.05	NEWARK	60	52 40	88/*79	0	(00	—	0.00
72.80	Claypole	—	55 58	86	—	6 19	76	4.75
78.45	Barkston S Junc	67	59 45	90/87	7	10 35	81	10.40
82.70	GRANTHAM	71	62 37	90	10	13 32	88	14.65
88.05	Stoke	75	66 15	86	14	17 21	85	20.00
99.50	Essendine	82	73 06	103	—	24 25	97/95	31.45
108.65	Werrington Junc	(†3)	78 40	*80	—	—	—	
111.80	PETERBOROUGH	94	82 08	*20	32½	32 20	98	43.75
118.80	Holme	—	88 55	*80	—	36 45	100/95	50.75
124.65	Abbots Ripton	—	92 55	88/84	—	40 16	100/92	56.60
129.30	HUNTINGDON	110	96 00	100	44	43 07	96	61.25
136.40	St Neots	—	100 28	94	—	47 22	102/98	68.35
144.00	Sandy	120	105 06	100	57	51 33	100	75.95
147.00	Biggleswade	(†3)	106 52	100/91	—	—	94	—
152.45	Three Counties	—	110 18	94/96	—	—	—	
156.25	HITCHIN	132	115 02	stop	65	59 13	98	88.20
	Stevenage (Old)	—	—	—	(†4)	61 23	95	91.60
	Woolmer Green	—	—	—	75½	64 40	99/95	96.60
	HATFIELD	—	—	—	82½	68 36	92	102.40
	Potters Bar	—	—	—	—	71 32	94	107.40
	Wood Green	—	—	—	92½	76 42	92/*80	115.15
						pws	*	
	Finsbury Park	—	—	—	—	79 42	Sigs*	117.60
	KINGS CROSS	—	—	—	99	85 48‡	sig stop	119.00

* Speed restriction   † Recovery time (min)   ‡ Sig stop outside Kings Cross

the stretch of fen beyond, No 55 003 was able to show a gain of more than 4min in some 30 miles. With its average of slightly over 95mph between Stoke and Wood Green, this was a beautifully judged piece of driving, with a punctual arrival at Kings Cross despite a signal stop between the tunnels to await platform clearance. Both the Pullman journeys were recorded by Mr Barrie.

Table 6 features running across the Plain of York between York and Darlington, for generations the traditional "racing ground" of the North Eastern and LNE Railways; this is practically level except for two faint rises at 1 in 629 for 6 miles northbound to Northallerton, and at 1 in 650 for 4 miles in the same direction towards Eryholme,

Table 6 (Runs 9 & 10)
ER YORK–DARLINGTON–NEWCASTLE

Locomotive: Type 55 Co-Co Diesel Load: coaches/tons tare/gross		9010 11, 385/410			55 001 11, 375/390		
Dist		Sched	Actual	Speeds	Sched	Actual	Speeds
miles		min	min sec	mph	min	min sec	mph
0.00	YORK	0	00 00	—	0	00 00	—
1.60	Skelton	3	2 56	57	4	3 55	54
5.55	Beningbrough	—	6 10	83	—	7 04	79
9.75	Tollerton	9	8 57	95	10½	10 03	88
16.10	Pilmoor	—	12 50	100	—	14 13	96
22.20	THIRSK	17	16 25	102	18½	18 05	92/96
29.95	NORTHALLERTON	22	21 01	101	23½	22 57	98/101
38.95	Eryholme	(†3) 31	26 20	99	—	28 12	99
41.55	Croft Spa	—	28 14	*75	—	29 53	96
						sigs	*46
44.10	DARLINGTON	37	32 05	—	32½	32 32	50
			stop			pass	
						pws	*29
49.55	Aycliffe				—	39 07	72/*67
54.25	Bradbury				—	42 33	86
57.00	Ferryhill				42	44 27	90
62.00	Croxdale				—	47 38	95/*80
66.15	DURHAM				49	50 50	*75
71.90	Chester-le-Street				—	54 30	99
74.70	Birtley				(†6)	56 15	95
77.70	Low Fell				—	58 09	85
79.60	King Ed Br Jc				65	60 30	*12
80.20	NEWCASTLE				67	62 41	stop
	Net time (min)		32		—	60	—

* Speed restriction   † Recovery time (min)

so that over the whole 44 mile course southbound trains have a slight advantage. Run No 9, recorded by Mr K. T. Budden, was remarkable both for its rapid initial acceleration and for the fast finish made possible by an absolutely clear road into the Darlington platform; the average speed over the 16.75 miles from Thirsk to Eryholme was 101.3mph. Run No 10, recorded by Mr Barrie on the "Aberdonian" with its non-stop run between York and Newcastle, is included principally to feature running between Darlington and Newcastle, a section which did not figure in the first edition. This journey was made during one of the worst gales of the 1975–76 winter, the fierce NW wind clearly hampering the locomotive on the very exposed stretch between Skelton and Northallerton. Nor was the driver of the "Aberdonian" able to secure full advantage from passing outside Darlington station on the through line, being checked by signals on the approach, and then suffering a long relaying slack beyond. But after the slowing for Aycliffe curves, and with the benefit of the re-alignment through Durham, an exhilarating sprint was made for home, with an average fractionally above 90mph over the 23.4 miles between Bradbury and Low Fell. With a very cautious approach, Newcastle was reached in a net time of 60min, at a net average speed of 80mph for the 80.20 miles.

In the reverse direction, Newcastle–York, the top half of Table 7

Table 7 (Runs Nos 11, 12, 13)
ER NEWCASTLE–DARLINGTON–YORK

Locomotive: Type 55 Co-Co Diesel No Load: coaches/tons tare/gross		55 010 (Run No 11) 9/305/320			55 006 (Run No 12) 11/378/395		
Dist		Sched	Actual	Speeds	Sched	Actual	Speeds
miles		min	min sec	mph	min	min sec	mph
0.00	NEWCASTLE	0	0 00	—	0	0 00	—
0.60	King Ed Br Jc	2	2 07	*	2	2 20	*
2.50	Low Fell	—	4 34	75	—	4 49	77
5.50	Birtley	—	6 41	88	—	6 51	95/100
8.30	Chester-le-Street	—	8 33	95	—	8 39	95
10.20	Plawsworth	—	9 46	85*/90	—	9 46	88/92
14.05	DURHAM	13	12 26	*70	14	12 25	*75
18.20	Croxdale	—	15 50	86/*73	—	15 42	88/*73
23.20	Ferryhill	20½	19 28	94	21½	19 30	85
25.95	Bradbury	—	21 11	100/106	—	21 19	92/100
30.65	Aycliffe	—	24 00	*70/90	—	24 10	*73
						pws	80/*19
36.10	DARLINGTON	30½	29 39	...	32½	32 31	—
—		—	See Note A	—	—	Net time 29½ min	
2.55	Croft Spa	—	4 25	69	—	3 40	70
5.15	Eryholme	7	6 31	76	—	5 43	82/77
14.15	NORTHALLERTON	13	12 34	93	11½	11 22	100/98
21.90	THIRSK	18	17 19	103	16½	16 00	102/99
28.00	Pilmoor	—	20 58	102	—	19 37	102
34.35	Tollerton	25½	24 42	101	24½	23 22	102/99
38.55	Beningbrough	—	27 13	100	—	25 52	102
42.50	Skelton	32	29 44	*	32½	28 14	*47
			sig stop	—			
44.10	YORK	35	37 16	—	36	32 11	stop
	Net time (min)	—	34	—	—	32	—

Note A: 9018 hauling 13 vehicles, 465/490 tons (Run No 13).
* Speed restriction

is occupied by two fast runs over the much-improved 36 miles between Newcastle and Darlington: the first, on the 14.50hrs Edinburgh–Kings Cross, being recorded by Mr P. A. Rutter and included in an article in *Modern Railways* for March, 1976, and the second by Mr Barrie on the preceding Aberdeen train. After the initial crawl over the King Edward Bridge, Up trains are able to get into stride very quickly down the east side of the Team Valley, as indicated in Runs 11 and 12. Both drivers also carried the ascent from Tyne Yard to beyond Plawsworth, partly at 1 in 198 and 1 in 150, in tremendous style until reducing speed for the passage of Durham station and over the "gable" past the now-demolished Relly Mill Junction. High speeds were resumed after the slack over Croxdale Viaduct, both trains topping the "century" beyond Bradbury; their overall times to the Darlington stop would have probably dead-heated were it not for the heavier train encountering a severe relaying slack beyond Aycliffe.

Across the Plain of York, many excellent runs are recorded daily, with very little difference in the times and speeds. In the first column of the Darlington–York table, the continuation of Mr Rutter's journey has been omitted in order to introduce a comparison between the 11-coach load of No 55 006 (Run 12) and one of 13 coaches, 465/490tons, hauled by No 9018 (Run 13) as timed by Mr K. T. Budden and published in the first edition. It will be seen that once No 9018 had got its 100 tons heavier load well on the move out of Darlington, there was only 18sec difference between the times of Nos 9018 and 55 006 over the 28.35 miles between Northallerton and Skelton, No 9018 averaging 101.6mph over this stretch with a gross load of nearly 500 tons.

The two runs over the East Coast main line between Newcastle and Edinburgh which are set in the final Table 8 are those which appeared in the first edition, recorded by Ronald I. Nelson (No 13) and J. B. Wearmouth (No 14) respectively. The reason why no later performance is recorded is that in 1975–76, up to 10min extra time was being allowed over this section for permanent way and signalling works necessary for future acceleration; even so, some of the running now tabulated was exciting enough. A gain of 20¼min gross and 22min net on the then operative 123min schedule, or of 17min net, and of substantial amounts of time with a 15-coach load of 538/575 tons, were fairly startling efforts. While the uphill work did not reach the level of that just described south of Doncaster, it was nevertheless of a high order, as witness the sustained 74mph up the 4 miles at 1 in 170 of Longhoughton bank, the acceleration from 56 to 68mph up the 1 in 190 from Berwick to milepost 53, and the 79–76mph up the

Table 8 (Runs Nos 13, 14)
ER & SCR NEW CASTLE—EDINBURGH

Locomotive: Type 55 Co-Co Diesel No Load: coaches/tons tare/gross		9011 13/462/485			9017 15/538/575		
Dist		Sched	Actual	Speeds	Sched	Actual	Speeds
miles		min	min sec	mph	min	min sec	mph
0·00	NEWCASTLE	0	0 00	—	0	0 00 sigs	— *15
2.70	Benton Bank	—	5 23	63	—	9 01	54
5.00	Forest Hall	—	7 36	64½	—	11 25	64
7.70	Annitsford	—	9 52	80½/77	—	14 43 pws	— *23
13.90	Stannington	—	14 23	89	—	21 51	82½
16.60	MORPETH	18	16 49	*40	18	24 17	*50
20.20	Longhirst	—	19 57	82	—	27 36	80/82
23.25	Widdrington	—	22 14	84	—	29 53	80/93
28.55	Acklington	—	25 45	92	—	33 33	92
31.95	Warkworth	—	28 10	*75/84	—	36 14	*68/83½
34.85	ALNMOUTH	33	30 23	*70/75	35	38 55	—
37.50	Longhoughton	—	32 29	74	—	4 36	52½
39.45	Little Mill	—	34 02	74	—	6 39	61½
43.15	Christon Bank	—	36 44	83½	—	9 35	92/96
46.15	Chathill	—	38 44	93	—	11 33	93/*77
51.65	BELFORD	47	42 38	80	16½	15 28	82
55.00	Smeafield	—	44 51 sigs	95½ *55	—	17 46	95/98
58.60	Beal	(†4)	47 49	67/79	(†3)	20 07	*87/92
63.60	Scremerston	—	51 42	77½	—	23 30	86
65.80	Tweedmouth	62½	53 46	*50	—	25 07	*60
67.00	BERWICK	—	54 49	56	34	26 49	—
71.45	Milepost 53	—	59 04	68	—	7 31	—
72.60	Burnmouth	—	60 01	74	—	8 32	70/*69
78.20	Reston Junc	75	64 22	79	—	13 13	74/68
83.30	Grantshouse	81	68 17	76	18	17 25	72/*66
88.00	Cockburnspath	—	71 53	86	—	21 20	80/*70
90.70	Innerwick	—	73 53	*	—	23 23	90
93.15	Oxwellmains	—	75 28	92½	—	25 03 sigs	— *30
95.35	DUNBAR	91	77 08	*60	29	28 53	—
101.05	East Linton	—	81 46	79/*72	—	—	—
106.70	DREM	101	85 40	91½/84	—	—	—
111.25	Longniddry	—	88 53	87	—	—	—
115.00	Prestonpans	—	91 29	86/89	—	—	—
118.35	Monktonhall Junc	111	94 05 pws	— *40	—	—	—
121.45	Portobello	117	97 53	*40	—	—	—
124.45	EDINBURGH	‡123	102 48	—	—	—	—

* Speed restriction   † Recovery time (min)   ‡ Since reduced to 118min

1 in 200 from Reston Junction to Grantshouse. There were momentary maximum speeds of 95½mph at Smeafield, and of 92–93mph at Acklington, Chathill, Oxwellmains and Drem, but otherwise nothing exceeding the 90mph "ceiling" then prevailing.

The exceptional feature of Run 14 was, of course, the load, the tare of the 15 coaches being 73 tons in excess of the 465 tons maximum laid down for this timing. Two bad checks resulted in a loss of 4min from Newcastle to the Alnmouth stop, but this was more than offset by the gain of 7¼min on the easy timing from Alnmouth to Berwick, and on the very tight timing of 29min from Berwick over Grantshouse Summit to Dunbar, 28.35 miles, the driver of No 9017 just held his own. This Deltic found no difficulty in maintaining speeds up to 90mph and slightly over on level track, but perhaps the most outstanding feat was to climb from Beal up past Scremerston, finishing with 2¾ miles at 1 in 190, without the speed dropping below 86mph. With a 575-ton load the time of no more than 26min 49sec start to stop over the 32.15 miles from Alnmouth to Berwick was notable indeed. With such performances the English Electric Deltic diesels have established an enviable record on the East Coast main line, and have proved themselves more than equal to every task that has been laid on them. They have surely established an outstanding record in the whole field of diesel-electric traction of their generation.

Names and Dimensions

Introduced
1961
Engines
Two 18-cyl. Napier "Deltic" 18–25 of
1,650bhp at 1,500rpm
Weight
100 tons
Maximum tractive effort
50,000lb

Total bhp
3,300
Transmission
Electric. Six English Electric EE750 25G
axle-hung   nose-suspended   traction
motors
Driving wheel diameter
3′ 7″

Original No	Final BR Class 55 No	
9000	55 022	*Royal Scots Grey*
9001	55 001	*St Paddy*
9002	55 002	*The King's Own Yorkshire Light Infantry*
9003	55 003	*Meld*
9004	55 004	*Queen's Own Highlander*
9005	55 005	*The Prince of Wales's Own Regiment of Yorkshire*
9006	55 006	*The Fife and Forfar Yeomanry*
9007	55 007	*Pinza*
9008	55 008	*The Green Howards*
9009	55 009	*Alycidon*
9010	55 010	*The King's Own Scottish Borderer*
9011	55 011	*The Royal Northumberland Fusiliers*
9012	55 012	*Crepello*
9013	55 013	*The Black Watch*
9014	55 014	*The Duke of Wellington's Regiment*
9015	55 015	*Tulyar*
9016	55 016	*Gordon Highlander*
9017	55 017	*The Durham Light Infantry*
9018	55 018	*Ballymoss*
9019	55 019	*Royal Highland Fusilier*
9020	55 020	*Nimbus*
9021	55 021	*Argyll and Sutherland Highlander*